W9-CDF-521

JULIAN H. GONZALEZ

THE CAPTAIN'S BRIGADE

Editor:
Tom Panzenhagen
Designer:
Jesus Maldonado
Photo editor:
Diane Weiss
Photo imaging:
Rose Ann McKean
Assistant editors:
Kevin Bull, Terrance Collins
Production editor:
Bob Ellis
Copy editors:
Bill Collison, Marisela delaGarza, Matt Fiorito, Maiya Hayes, Tim Marcinkoski, Mary Masson, Steve Schrader, Al Toby and the Free Press sports copy desk
Cover design:
Ryan Ford
Cover photo:
David Gilkey
Project coordinator:
Dave Robinson
Special thanks to:
Steve Dorsey, John Fleming, Mark Francescutti, Gene Myers, Mike Thompson

Detroit Free Press

600 W. Fort St.
Detroit, MI 48226
©2006 by Detroit Free Press. All rights reserved.

Manufactured by Quebecor World Dubuque, United States of America.

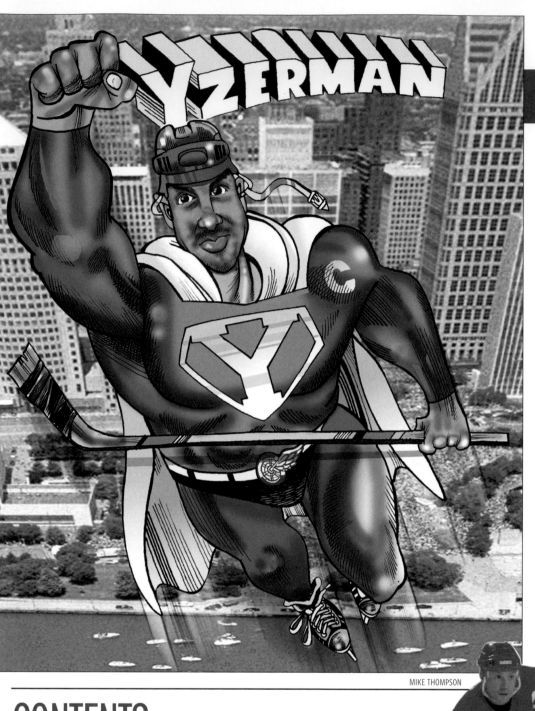

MIKE THOMPSON

CONTENTS

"I did the best I could." The Captain, at his farewell news conference, July 3, 2006

1997 JUNE 7

1998 JUNE 16

2002 JUNE 13

2006 JULY 3

CAPTAIN FOREVER

CUP IN HAND: Yzerman
flashes a gap-toothed smile
as he hoists the Stanley
Cup for the first time.
MARY SCHROEDER

From the day he was drafted, a shaggy-haired kid with a soft, nervous voice, he promised to do his best, even though, as he warned a TV interviewer, he sometimes tried to do too much. Who knew that sentence would be an understatement? He did so much for his team and his town that in time it became immeasurable — and impossible to reproduce. Steve Yzerman, the man, has retired as a hockey player and will go on with his life.

BY MITCH ALBOM
2006
JULY 3

But Steve Yzerman, the idea, is likely gone for good.

Captain Forever has hung up his skates after months of speculation, and we will not see the likes of him again: A guy who plays more than two decades in one city, who leads the team practically the entire time, who comes to embody the uniform, the building, the halls, the very ice itself. It is no lie to say his face could have been imprinted on our city limits, and his jersey has been worn by more Detroiters than any shirt, shoe or tie. If you live in this town you know where you were when Steve Yzerman hoisted that first Stanley Cup over his head at center ice, flashing the gap in his teeth. You remember him waving in the parade car. And it didn't matter where you were the day he retired — at work, at home, Up North for the Fourth of July holiday — when you heard the news, it hit you the same way.

The Red Wings actually will take the ice without No. 19. He won't be injured. He won't be on his way back.

He'll be watching, like the rest of us.

Captain Forever skates no more.

"I almost feel like a little boy trying to please his parents every time I step on the ice the way the fans here support the team," he said at a Joe Louis

JULIAN H. GONZALEZ

CHAMPAGNE SHAMPOO: A fan douses Yzerman with bubbly in the locker room on June 7, 1997, after the Wings swept Philadelphia to win their first Stanley Cup in 42 years. By then, Yzerman had been playing for the Wings for 14 seasons, 11 as captain.

Arena news conference.

And that is an apt description for how those fans feel today: like their little boy has grown up, moved out, taken that job that really, truly moves him out of the house.

But let us be careful here. Steve Yzerman did not stop living. He just stopped playing. And this should be a celebration, not a memorial. He came into the game with a dream of being the best, and he leaves the game not over drama, age, contracts, money, management or even the old chestnut "I want to spend more time with

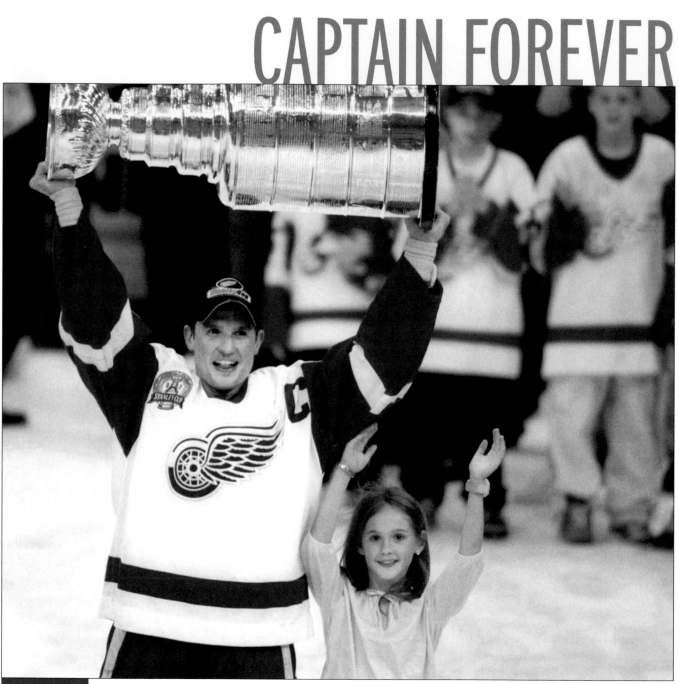

KIRTHMON F. DOZIER

DADDY-DAUGHTER DANCE: With 8-year-old daughter Isabella mimicking his every move, Yzerman hoists the Stanley Cup for a third time, on June 13, 2002. In the finals, the Red Wings had beaten Carolina in five games, and it was the first time under Captain Steve the team could celebrate the title on home ice.

Twenty-two seasons, three Cups, 10 All-Star teams

my family."

He leaves the game because of the same reason he got into it, the dream of being the best. That dream, on the ice, is finally, sadly no longer realistic.

He said so. He said he questioned his ability to do what he always had done. Too many injuries. Too many miles. He said he had become "a part-time player." Analysts have said similar things, but true warrior athletes never hear any voices but their own.

When that voice speaks, they listen.

Captain Forever skates no more.

So Yzerman, after 22 seasons, three Stanley Cups, 10 All-Star teams, one Olympic gold medal, countless swooning females, endless beer-bellied supporters and more surgeries and rehabs than any man should have to endure, made his announcement with the people who brought him to this city around him: Mike Ilitch, the owner, and Jimmy Devellano, who drafted him in 1983.

But there were other things around him, too, in the air, over his shoulder, between his words, dodging his gestures, the spray of memories and stories that his name instantly stirs up for any fan of this team or this beautiful game of hockey.

Here are a few of mine:

There's Steve Yzerman on an early morning in the late 1980s, heading to his car at the airport, after the upstart Wings lost the conference finals to the then mighty Edmonton Oilers. "They're not so tough," young Yzerman says, his eyes on the future.

There's Steve Yzerman racking up huge numbers, scoring like a machine, being hailed as one of the top three players of his time — and his time includes Wayne Gretzky and Mario Lemieux.

There's Steve Yzerman consulting with Jacques Demers, who loves him, and Bryan Murray, who loves him, and Scotty Bowman, who loves him, and Dave Lewis, who loves him, and Mike Babcock, who can't help but love him, too.

There's Steve Yzerman slamming into a goal post, being helped off the ice. There's Yzerman going down as if shot, a puck having missed his eye by millimeters.

There's Steve Yzerman getting married.

MARY SCHROEDER

DOWN AND ICY: Yzerman always was one of the Wings' gutsiest players. Here he battles Toronto's Doug Gilmour for position to get control of the puck.

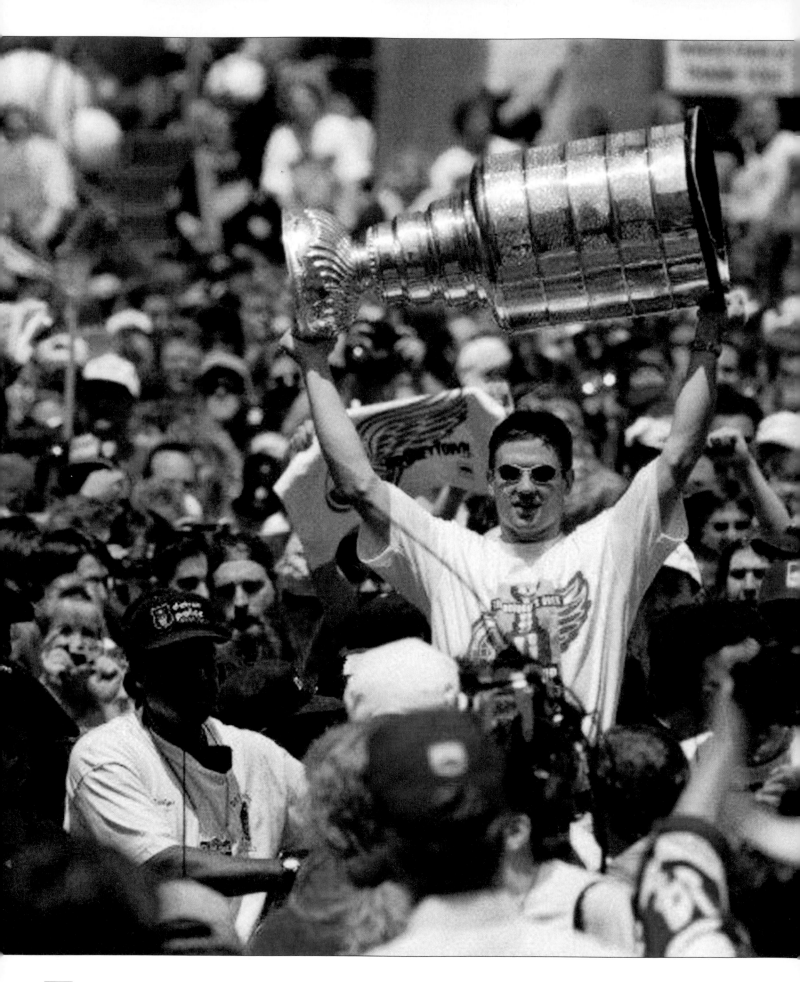

CAPTAIN FOREVER

His right knee is beyond bad. You swear it only works because it must be connected to his heart.

There he is having his first child, a girl, and his second, a girl, and his third, a girl. There he is with long hair, with shorter hair, with thinning hair. There he is with a black eye, with stitched lips, with new scars on his Johnny Depp face.

There he is, spring after lonely spring, in the losers' locker room, going home too early, sweating through a black polo shirt one year, a checkered sports coat another year — why can I remember these details? — explaining why his team lost too soon, too early, what went wrong, speaking somberly, blankly, wondering if he's ever going to win a championship.

And there he is winning that championship in 1997, soaked in champagne in the steaming, packed Joe Louis Arena locker room, hugging everybody, smiling at everything, croaking a sentence that revealed all he had hidden all those empty years. His voice is raspy. He seems near tears. "They always say, 'He's a good player, but he didn't win it.' And now they can't say that anymore."

He looks in our eyes. "No matter what, they can't say it, you know?"

We knew. He knew. The world knew.

At that moment, you really did believe Captain Forever could live up to the name.

But men age, skates dull, time passes and decisions are made. This is the right one. The fact is, fans had wondered if Yzerman might call it quits as early as 2002, after his last Stanley Cup. Many close to him thought he might

leave after the 2004 season, what with his eye injury and the labor stoppage that followed.

Yes, we saw a surge of the old Yzerman down the home stretch of the 2005-06 season, as he approached his 41st birthday. And yes, for the bleak one round of playoffs, he was the Wings' gutsiest — if not their best — player.

But it was painful for him to go out there and it was becoming painful to watch — at least for those who loved his legend and wanted it unscratched. His right knee is beyond bad. You swear it only works because it must be connected to his heart.

So he pulls off the sweater and they take the name off his locker and they retire his number and anything else they can think of. Yzerman has never been into that stuff. Outsiders may not understand why Detroit had such an infatuation with this guy, but it's because he symbolizes the way we feel, the way we approach things and the way we dream. He played hockey, not the biggest of sports, and he was 5-feet-11, not the biggest of guys, and he played in Detroit, not the biggest of cities.

But he dreamed big. And he never stopped trying. And he never lost his humility. And finally, 14 years after he joined his company, at an age when other guys already have given it up, he saw his big dream come true.

And that's what we want for ourselves. That's what working-class people fantasize when they drop their heads on the pillow: a chance for it all to come true. It is

MOTOWN MANIA: Yzerman, appropriately, is at the center of things as a throng estimated at one million parade downtown to celebrate Detroit's first Stanley Cup in 42 years on June 10, 1997.

CRAIG PORTER

SEE YOU IN THE HALL OF FAME: Yzerman greets former coach Scotty Bowman before The Captain's farewell news conference. Together they brought Detroit three Stanley Cups.

He dreamed big. And he saw his big dream come true.

the reason why there have been and will be many athletes in Detroit who will be called "Captain." But only one will get a "The" in front.

And that's the difference.

That's all the difference.

"I did the best I could," he said.

This was his humble summation, and it was pretty much what he promised when he came here. So in the end, Steve Yzerman is, above all things, a man of his word, and his word was good and he was good and the idea of him was good.

Better than good.

It was the best of ideas, when you think about it, one man in one place for one team in one city, saying good-bye and witnessing, in return, a sea of admirers in a farewell salute worthy of a captain. ●

THE CAPTAIN'S LOG

On June 8, 1983, at the Montreal Forum, the Red Wings drafted Steve Yzerman, an 18-year-old center from the Peterborough Petes of the Ontario Hockey League. Yzerman was the fourth pick – after Brian Lawton, Sylvain Turgeon and Pat LaFontaine. Yzerman retired July 3, 2006, leaving as the longest-serving captain in NHL history after 19 seasons in charge. He ranks sixth all-time in points, seventh in assists and eighth in goals.

 1984
 1986
 1995
 2005

YEAR-BY-YEAR STATISTICS

SEASON	GAMES	POINTS	Goals	Assists	PLAYOFF RESULTS
1983-84	80	87	39	48	Lost division semifinals to St. Louis
1984-85	80	89	30	59	Lost division semifinals to Chicago
1985-86	51	42	14	28	Did not make playoffs
1986-87	80	90	31	59	Lost conference finals to Edmonton
1987-88	64	102	50	52	Lost conference finals to Edmonton
1988-89	80	155	65	90	Lost division semifinals to Chicago
1989-90	79	127	62	65	Did not make playoffs
1990-91	80	108	51	57	Lost division semifinals to St. Louis
1991-92	79	103	45	58	Lost division finals to Chicago
1992-93	84	137	58	79	Lost division semifinals to Toronto
1993-94	58	82	24	58	Lost conference quarters to San Jose
1994-95	47	38	12	26	Lost Stanley Cup finals to New Jersey
1995-96	80	95	36	59	Lost conference finals to Colorado
1996-97	81	85	22	63	**WON STANLEY CUP (vs. Philadelphia)**
1997-98	75	69	24	45	**WON STANLEY CUP (vs. Washington)**
1998-99	80	74	29	45	Lost conference semifinals to Colorado
'99-2000	78	79	35	44	Lost conference semifinals to Colorado
2000-01	54	52	18	34	Lost conference quarters to Los Angeles
2001-02	52	48	13	35	**WON STANLEY CUP (vs. Carolina)**
2002-03	16	8	2 goals, 6 assists		Lost conference quarters to Anaheim
2003-04	75	51	18	33	Lost conference semifinals to Calgary
2004-05	–	–	Season locked out		No playoffs
2005-06	61	34	14	20	Lost conference quarters to Edmonton
TOTALS	**1,514**	**1,755**	**692 goals, 1,063 assists**		

Sources: www.nhl.com; Free Press research

Graphic by JOHN W. FLEMING/Detroit Free Press; photos from Free Press files

IN THE BEGINNING

BEFORE HE WAS THE CAPTAIN

"I was excited – I never felt any burden at 18. I just wanted to play in the league."
Yzerman, on being drafted by the Wings

COURTESY RED WINGS

WELCOME: Yzerman shakes hands with owner Mike Ilitch after the Red Wings drafted him fourth overall in 1983. The Wings had intended to draft Pat LaFontaine, but the New York Islanders grabbed him with the third pick.

When Steve Yzerman arrived in Detroit in 1983, he was 18, had a layer of baby fat, the makings of a mullet, and he ordered white milk in bars.

BY BILL McGRAW   The lady who housed him in junior hockey said at the time: "He always took his plates to the sink."

His career turned out to be a fairy tale, but back then, before all the nifty goals, painful injuries, Stanley Cups and furniture commercials, Yzerman was an unknown.

And the supreme irony is the Red Wings didn't really want him at first.

In 1983, new owner Mike Ilitch and general manager Jimmy Devellano saw one player in that year's amateur draft who they believed would do wonders for the moribund franchise they were desperately trying to resuscitate.

That player was Pat LaFontaine, the charismatic center from Waterford Township, who had just completed a spectacular junior career in Quebec.

"He was a local boy who would have been a super marketing tool," Devellano recalled. "We had 4,000 season-ticket owners and had just missed the playoffs (for the fifth year in a row). The cupboard was bare."

But the New York Islanders, drafting third, chose LaFontaine, who went on to have a Hall of Fame career.

The next choice belonged to the Wings. Devellano took Yzerman, and suddenly Yzerman assumed the role of being Ilitch's main building block when he should have been making plans for the senior prom.

"I was excited — I never felt any burden at 18," Yzerman said at his retirement news conference. "I just wanted to play in the league. And I had no idea if I could play in the league."

He made an impression from the first day of training camp.

"After one session, you knew he was a tremendous hockey player," said Ken Holland, the Wings' general manager who was a minor-league goalie for Detroit in 1983.

During the regular season, Yzerman centered the Wings' top line and quickly caught the eye of Joe Louis Arena crowds with his on-ice intelligence and quick moves.

He scored in his first game and ended his rookie year with 39 goals and 48 assists.

"He represented the turning-of-the-page for the franchise," said Colin Campbell, the NHL's director of hockey operations, who was one of the Wings' veterans in 1983.

As a youngster, Yzerman was shy and quiet and kept a low profile off the ice. He treated the older players — who were nowhere near his equal when it came to talent — with respect.

"He was even a better person than a player," Campbell said.

Yzerman scored 229 goals in his first six seasons. Coach Jacques Demers appointed him captain in 1986, and the media and fans began comparing him to such contemporary Detroit superstars as Alan Trammell and Isiah Thomas.

In 1988-89, Yzerman scored 65 goals and 90 assists, and the Wings had evolved into a truly interesting — if not a truly contending — team.

At the start of that season, speculating on the future, Yzerman said: "I'd like to stay in Detroit my entire career. I don't know what's going to happen, whether they want me or not."

He added: "But I know I don't want to go anywhere else." Ⓒ

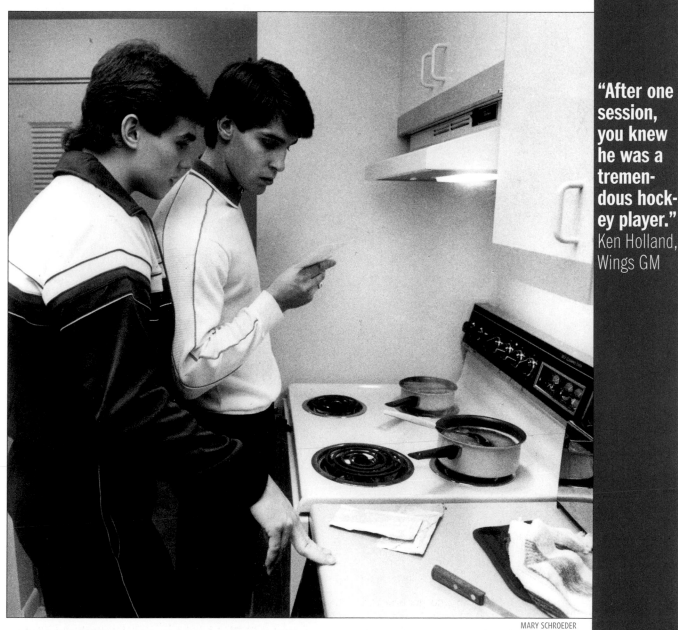

"After one session, you knew he was a tremendous hockey player."
Ken Holland, Wings GM

MARY SCHROEDER

WHAT'S COOKING? Yzerman shared an apartment with fellow Red Wing Lane Lambert, right. Here they are preparing a nutritious lunch of hot dogs with macaroni and cheese.

SLAP-SHOT SNAPSHOT: Yzerman practices his shot. In 1983-84, he led NHL rookies in assists with 48 and in points with 87. He was second in goals with 39, behind only Hartford's Sylvain Turgeon (40).
FILE PHOTO

'HE'S READY TO PLAY'

"He always looked dangerous. That tells you something, especially on the road."
Coach Nick Polano

BY BILL McGRAW

1983
OCTOBER 5

WINNIPEG, Manitoba — The Red Wings displayed some promising sides to their new selves in their season opener — a splendid evening by rookie Steve Yzerman; a teamwide, gung-ho effort, and good goaltending by Eddie Mio.

The Red Wings even came from behind three times, but they didn't win.

They didn't lose, either.

They tied the Winnipeg Jets, 6-6, and escaped with a point on the road, five-minute overtime and all.

"Anytime you get a point against one of the top teams, and considering it's on the road, there were a lot of good signs," said Detroit captain Danny Gare.

The Wings had a 6-5 lead with less

than four minutes to play, and it might have been a perfect evening for Yzerman had the score stood up.

He made the play on the sixth Detroit goal by taking the puck into the Jets' zone and scooting around defenseman Bob Dollas, who, like Yzerman, was a first-round draft choice.

Yzerman brought the puck in on goalie Doug Soetaert, where Eddie Johnstone was lurking, and Johnstone scored.

"Steve made a hell of a play," Johnstone said. "I was just going for the net."

Yzerman had scored himself earlier, in the first period, giving the Wings a 3-1 lead. That time, he fought off two checks and skated diagonally through the Jets' zone and scored on his own

rebound.

He also looked smart on the power play and hardly seemed 18 years old.

Afterward, Yzerman admitted he wasn't totally happy with his first NHL game.

"I was kind of disappointed with my defensive play," he said. "And I was disappointed with my face-offs. I had little lapses. I'm always learning, and I want to cut down on my mistakes each game."

When pressed, he added: "It was one of my better games."

"It was a great game for Steve," teammate Paul Woods said

Said Coach Nick Polano: "He always looked dangerous. That tells you something, especially on the road. This was a good test for Steve. He showed us he's ready to play." ◓

MEET THE RED WINGS

The team during Yzerman's rookie season, 1983-84 (Nick Polano coach, Dan Belisle assistant coach), with comments culled from a Free Press preview of the 1984 playoffs:

▮ **Pierre Aubry, forward, 23:** Biggest thrill was a fishing trip in northern Quebec, would like to be an accountant.

▮ **John Barrett, defense, 26:** Makes his home in Ottawa, and says he'd probably farm there if he wasn't playing hockey.

▮ **Ivan Boldirev, forward, 34:** Biggest disappointment was not going to college.

▮ **Colin Campbell, defense, 31:** He and his wife have three children, who he says are his biggest thrill.

▮ **Ron Duguay, forward, 26:** Recently married model Robin Bobo.

▮ **Blake Dunlop, forward, 30:** Missing his daughter's birth while on the road was his biggest disappointment.

▮ **Dwight Foster, forward, 27:** Biggest disappointment was lending his best man $300 and never being paid back.

▮ **Danny Gare, forward, 29:** The captain before Yzerman, his biggest thrill is having two healthy daughters.

▮ **Ed Johnstone, forward, 30:** Lives to fish for trout in the Northwest Territory, says his biggest disappointment is not being 6-3 and 225 pounds (he's 5-9, 187).

▮ **Kelly Kisio, forward, 24:** Biggest thrill was watching his son's birth, enjoys golf and fishing.

▮ **Randy Ladouceur, defense, 23:** Enjoys fishing, swimming and water skiing.

▮ **Lane Lambert, forward, 19:** Biggest disappointment was losing in the finals of the Canadian Midget Softball championships.

▮ **Reed Larson, defense, 27:** Biggest thrill was beating teammate Paul Woods in a summer fishing derby.

▮ **Claude Loiselle, forward, 20:** Would be a carpenter if he wasn't playing hockey.

▮ **Rick MacLeish, forward, 34:** After hockey, says he plans to not work for the rest of his life.

▮ **Bob Manno, forward, 27:** Biggest thrill was a hole-in-one.

▮ **Barry Melrose, defense, 27:** Owns a farm in Kelvington, Saskatchewan.

▮ **Corrado Micalef, goalie, 22:** Would like to be a lawyer if he wasn't playing hockey.

▮ **Ed Mio, goalie, 30:** Says he'd be working in an automobile factory if he wasn't playing hockey.

▮ **John Ogrodnick, forward, 25:** Enjoys fishing and water skiing.

▮ **Brad Park, defense, 35:** Most exciting playoff experience was scoring a winning goal for Boston against Buffalo in 1983.

▮ **Joe Paterson, forward, 23:** Enjoys white water rafting on the Ottawa River.

▮ **Greg Smith, defense, 28:** Was a teammate of Ed Mio's at Colorado College.

▮ **Greg Stefan, goalie, 23:** Was a childhood teammate of Wayne Gretzky's in Brantford, Ontario.

▮ **Paul Woods, forward, 28:** Biggest thrill was the first time he and his father used a chainsaw. Biggest disappointment? When the saw ran out of gas.

▮ **Steve Yzerman, forward, 18:** Says his biggest thrill was graduating from high school, would be going to Grade 13 or college if he wasn't playing hockey.

18 GOING ON 19

"He's got tremendous poise. And tremendous natural ability."
Teammate Brad Park

RICHARD LEE

HAIR APPARENT: Yzerman's career spanned the eras of hockey: Here he skates with Ron Duguay, one of the last NHL players not to wear a helmet. Yzerman and Duguay played together in 1983-86, before Duguay was traded to Pittsburgh.

Steve Yzerman is so young that he remembers scoring his first goal as if it was yesterday. Actually, he got it about 13 years ago — when he was 5 — while playing his first season of organized hockey in western Canada. It was not a pretty sight.

BY BILL McGRAW

1983

NOVEMBER 8

"I couldn't even stand up," Yzerman said. "I had fallen down in front of the net. Their guy banked it off one of their guys' skates and into the net. I was lying there, and I got credit for it."

How times have changed. Yzerman has begun his rookie season in superb fashion. He is quick, smart and sometimes sensational on the ice. He is centering the Wings' top line and is as responsible as anyone for the club's fine start, which has drawn huge, enthusiastic crowds to Joe Louis Arena.

As the first player drafted by general manager Jimmy Devellano, Yzerman appears to be a fine cornerstone for a rebuilt franchise. And he is doing all this at age 18, just a few months out of high school.

Born May 9, 1965, Yzerman is one of the NHL's youngest players, and he is easily the baby among Detroit's major league pro athletes. But his age is deceiving, because Yzerman acts 18 going on 28. To the adults he deals with daily, he is a fellow adult, an old pro with a kid's face.

"He came into camp low-key," said teammate Danny Gare. "He listens a lot. He takes a lot in. You see him watching things. He was very confident but very quiet."

"He's got tremendous poise," said Brad Park. "And tremendous natural ability."

Yzerman's father, Ron, a social worker who is director of welfare services for the Canadian government, said Steve always seemed a bit older than his age.

"He just sort of developed a sophistication and probably matured a little quicker," Ron Yzerman said.

On Steve's hockey-playing trips as a youth, Ron said, the family would do more than watch hockey. They would visit the towns "to see how other people lived. That sort of contributed to his socialization," Ron said.

As a child, Steve defused a potentially touchy family situation, Ron recalled, when he refused to flaunt his hockey ability after it had surpassed that of his older brother, Mike.

"He never said, 'I'm better, I deserve the better skates,' that sort of thing," his father said. "I think it was a conscious decision on his part."

"He thought of other people ahead of himself," said Lottie Garvey, who houses hockey players in Peterborough, Ontario. Yzerman lived with the Garveys for two years while starring for the Peterborough Petes junior team.

Yzerman was born in Cranbrook, British Columbia, where the family's favorite NHL club was the Red Wings. They moved to suburban Ottawa while Steve was still in grade school.

In Detroit, Yzerman shares a suburban home with fellow rookie Lane Lambert, 19.

At 18, Yzerman says he is still the small-town kid from Cranbrook, Ottawa and Peterborough, no matter how many goals he scores, no matter how much he captivates the big city.

"I just plan on being the same way," he said. "I don't plan on changing. I hope people like me and appreciate me the way I am." ⊙

MARY SCHROEDER

CLEAN-CUT KID: Yzerman does his laundry in his digs at the Riverfront Apartments in Detroit in this 1984 photo. The building was just west of Yzerman's place of business: Joe Louis Arena.

RHYMES WITH ICERMAN

During his rookie season, it wasn't unusual to see a certain parenthetical phrase in stories about Steve Yzerman: "(pronounced EYE-zer-man)."

Mike Downey, then a Free Press sports columnist, wrote the following in 1983:

It was her first time.

She had never been to a hockey game before. "I don't know anything about this game," she said.

"Leave it to me, baby," I said. "I'm a big-time sports writer. I know all about this stuff."

We took our seats. I asked the guy behind me which team was Detroit and which team was Pittsburgh. Steve Yzerman did something good for Detroit. The public-address announcer announced his name and the crowd cheered. She thought it was cute that his name sounded like Icerman.

"From reading it in the paper," she said, "I thought it was Yizzerman."

BABY FACE

BY GEORGE
PUSCAS

1984

MARCH 21

You pause a moment in the Red Wings locker room to consider the rising fortunes of this team, and quickly you notice something strange: A bare-chested kid is standing by the wall. He is surrounded by television cameras and characters with tape recorders and notebooks in hand.

They are asking him questions, and he is replying as if he were a sage of hockey, or at least like a guy who knows what he's talking about.

This is Steve Yzerman. He's 18 years old. If the kid shaves, it's only for practice.

There's no evidence it has happened, but it's 8-to-1 if somebody in the Red Wings locker room hollered, "Hey, kid, pick up all those towels and sweep the floor," Yzerman might jump.

Eighteen, for gosh sakes, is a time when most young fellas are still learning to comb their hair and match their socks. They're sweating algebra and chasing cheerleaders in high school. It's an age that doesn't count for much of anything unless, of course, there's a war on.

You never expect an 18-year-old to be an important element in a grown-up world. Especially professional sports. It happens rarely in baseball or basketball, never in football.

There was a time in hockey, not all that long ago, when the ugliest guys in a locker room were not the sports writers but the players. When the players would take out their teeth

YZERKID: As an 18-year-old rookie, Yzerman was described as "baby-cheeked" by Detroit Free Press sports columnist George Puscas.

and grin, the scars would stretch out over the wrinkles in their worn faces. They scared the hell out of each other.

Now you look around and there's a baby-cheeked Steve Yzerman and a Lane Lambert, who's 19. And there's Pat LaFontaine, 19, with the champion New York Islanders.

You wonder what is happening in hockey, that guys so young they can't buy a legal beer can make it so big and so quickly in a game where men always prevailed.©

MATINEE IDOLS

BY PATRICIA CHARGOT

Hundreds came to Joe Louis Arena from St. Clair Shores, Sterling Heights, Port Huron, Dearborn and Windsor to stand in line for several hours in the early-morning cold to buy tickets for the first Red Wings playoff games since 1978.

There were young married couples from the suburbs.

Some of the women, pushing babies in strollers, said they came to support their husbands, even though the husbands, who had called in sick to work, were not planning to take their wives to the big games.

There were teenage boys, all of whom had skipped school. Most were buying tickets for themselves and their fathers.

There were two sisters, who

also said they had skipped school, with serious crushes on Ron Duguay and Steve Yzerman.

"Dad said, 'You better not go down there to get those tickets,' " said Pam, 15.

"But mom knows," said Carolyn, 18. "This is our last chance to get a glance of Duguay and Yzerman."

The sisters became Wings

fans "when Pam started listening to the games because she heard Duguay was coming to Detroit and saw his picture," Carolyn said.

Pam: "Then I started liking Yzerman, after seeing him play."

Carolyn: "They're both really good-looking."

Pam: "Yeah, but I love Steve."

ROOKIE CARD

MARY SCHROEDER

LINEUP: Yzerman, center, is flanked by teammates after a rigorous workout. Yzerman, 18, regarded defenseman Brad Park, right, as an old-timer at 35.

Steve Yzerman's rookie season ended April 8, 1984, when the St. Louis Blues eliminated the Red Wings from the playoffs. Yzerman, who led all NHL rookies in scoring during the season, led the Wings in the playoffs with three goals and three assists in four games.

◆ ◆ ◆

As a kid, Yzerman's hockey role models did not include Gordie Howe. His favorites were Bryan Trottier — that's where he got the No. 19 — and Mike Bossy of the Islanders. His rookie stats are comparable to the two Islanders all-stars, who both won the Calder Trophy as rookie of the year.

Yzerman finished his first season with 39 goals, 48 assists for 87 points. In Trottier's rookie year, 1975-76, he had 32-63 for 95 points. Bossy had 53-38 for 91 points in 1977-78.

◆ ◆ ◆

Yzerman was chosen by the NHL players as The Sporting News rookie of the year. He received 162 of a possible 313 votes. "I'm very happy about it," he said. "It's nice being recognized like this by your fellow players." His closest competitor with 83 votes was Buffalo goalie Tom Barrasso, who would win the Calder Trophy, based on voting by members of the Professional Hockey Writers Association. ◖

CAPTAIN DETROIT
COMEBACK KID
STEVIE WONDERFUL
'A PURE RED WING'
BOYS' NIGHT OUT
THE END OF THE BEGINNING

CAPTAIN DETROIT

"The captain has to be a guy who can play, a guy who on and off the ice shows some class." Red Wings coach Jacques Demers

JULIAN H. GONZALEZ

STAYING POWER: Steve Yzerman, a Red Wing for 22 seasons, first donned the "C" as a 21-year-old, which made him the youngest captain in club history. He remained in that role until his retirement in 2006, becoming known simply as "The Captain."

MARY SCHROEDER

LONG TERM: Coach Jacques Demers said he wanted to choose a captain capable of wearing the "C" for many years. The new captain, flanked above by Paul MacLean, left, and Adam Oates, promised to be a quiet leader.

Red Wings coach Jacques Demers named Steve Yzerman team captain on Oct. 7, 1986. Demers presented Yzerman, the 21-year-old center, with a Wings sweater bearing the "C" at a news conference after practice at Oak Park Ice Arena. Yzerman, in his fourth NHL season, became the youngest captain in the Wings' 61-year history. He succeeded Danny Gare, who was released after the 1985-86 season and acquired by Edmonton.

BY KEITH GAVE

Two weeks before Yzerman received the "C," Free Press hockey writer Keith Gave filed the following report.

Sometime soon, Jacques Demers will call Steve Yzerman aside, shake his hand and pin the captain's "C" on his Red Wings sweater. It will be a significant moment, Demers said, because he considers picking a captain one of the most important decisions he will make this season.

"I want to be very careful on this assignment," Demers said. "I want to be sure whoever it is is capable of wearing the 'C' for many years to come.

"Steve Yzerman seems to fit the bill

"The captain has to be a guy who can play," Demers said, "a guy who on and off the ice shows some class; a guy who wears the Detroit Red Wings sweater with some pride; and a guy who the other players look up to and respect. He doesn't have to necessarily be a rah-rah guy but someone who will stand up when times get tough and say, 'Let's go, guys, this is it.'

"And he has to be able to see the coach's side as well as the players' side. There's a lot of pressure."

Before this, Yzerman would have been a surprise choice. The 21-year-old center had been one of the most reserved players in the dressing room in his previous three NHL seasons, and his detractors said he

was too preoccupied with extracurricular social activities to worry about his teammates. But he has matured tremendously.

Yzerman was coming off a dreadful season in 1985-86, in which he was injured. In 51 games, he scored 14 goals and suddenly was confronted by a vulnerability he had never known.

"Last year, I had a lot of things going" off the ice, Yzerman said. "I bought a house, got a new contract and I was starting to enjoy things a bit. Then, having a bad season made me more aware of what it's really all about.

"I've always had my confidence, even through last year. But I know I've got to prove a lot to a lot of people. I can't afford another year like last year."

Yzerman said he hopes to be a quiet leader. "I'm not a real vocal guy or anything," he said. "I'd try to do it by working hard, by being a good example." ©

> **"I'm not a real vocal guy or anything. I'd try to do it by working hard, by being a good example."**
> Yzerman, on being captain

COMEBACK KID

"It isn't an award I was ever thinking about. I'm sure I'll hear about it from the old guys on the team, like Dave Lewis." Yzerman, on winning Comeback Player of the Year

MARY SCHROEDER

TALE OF A TURNAROUND: In 1985-86, Yzerman missed the last 29 games of the season because of a broken collarbone. In 1987, he was back on the ice, mixing it up against guys like Troy Murray of the Chicago Blackhawks. His return prompted The Hockey News to name him Comeback Player of the Year. Yzerman was all of 21 years old.

After a disappointing 1985-86 season shortened by injury, Yzerman rebounded with 31 goals and 90 points the next season.

BY MITCH ALBOM

1987
APRIL 17

Aw, come on. The guy doesn't even shave. Comeback Player of the Year? Steve Yzerman?

The one with the Reebok sneakers and the jeans and the face off a teen magazine cover? That Steve Yzerman?

How old is he? Nine?

"Twenty-one," he says, shyly, sipping a Coke.

Twenty-one? Ho. Did he really say 21? Well. OK. Comeback Player of the Year. Twenty-one. What's next? Retirement? Maybe each team will give him a clock or an oil painting or a rocking chair on his final visit.

And the book. He can write the book. Then the movie.

Twenty-one. Comeback Player of the Year.

Now I know that hockey is a young sport. I have walked through the Red Wings locker room. I have seen Shawn Burr, who cannot drink in certain states, and Joe Kocur, who could borrow Burr's ID.

They look young.

They might ride a school bus to practice.

But none of them won Comeback Player of the Year.

"It did kind of surprise me," Yzerman says, of the announcement by The Hockey News that he, Darren Veitch, 26, and Brian Hayward, 26, had been selected — one forward, one defenseman, one goalie.

"It isn't an award I was ever thinking about. I'm sure I'll hear about it from the old guys on the team, like Dave Lewis."

Lewis, "the old guy," is 33. ⊖

STEVIE WONDERFUL

KIRTHMON F. DOZIER

SAINT STEVIE: His chiseled features and deep brown eyes caused a few hearts to flutter around Michigan — and if his handsome face didn't hook you, his nice-guy reputation might. In 22 years with the Red Wings, he became one of the city's most beloved sports heroes.

> "I would never just go up to Gordie Howe out of the blue. ... What am I gonna say, 'Hey, Gordie. How's it goin'?' "
> Yzerman

BY MITCH ALBOM

1988
DECEMBER 9

You want to know my biggest fear about Steve Yzerman? That success will one day grab him by the neck and say, "Look, kid, wake up. You're a star. Stop treating people so nicely!"

It could happen. Plenty of athletes begin humble and wind up haughty. It's easy when the whole city is fawning over you. And yet it is tough to fawn over Yzerman. He likes to hide in the woods of normality.

The other day I called him up. I said, "What are you doing?" He said, "Nothing. My fiancée is at a Tupperware party."

A Tupperware party?

He made a commercial for Ford recently. Didn't use an agent. Just went in, heard the offer and accepted it. ("Well, it's not like I'd won any Oscars," Yzerman says. "I couldn't really demand anything.")

He recently eclipsed a Detroit hockey record held by the great Gordie Howe, most consecutive games with at least one goal — nine. *(Editor's note: It's a feat Yzerman would repeat in 1992, and the record stood at the time of his retirement in 2006.)*

I ask whether he has ever met Howe.

"A couple of times," he says. "He'll come over and say hi."

"Couldn't you just say hello first?"

His eyes bulge.

"No way! I would never just go up to Gordie Howe out of the blue."

"Why not?"

"Because he's Gordie Howe. What am I gonna say, 'Hey, Gordie. How's it goin'?'"

"Well, don't you think you've reached that point?"

He shakes his head.

"I'll never reach that point."

Now. Whoa. This is not Butch Deadmarsh

STEVIE WONDERFUL

"There's no comparison between Wayne Gretzky and me. He's done it all. Won Stanley Cups, won scoring championships." Yzerman

talking. This is a guy who many believe is the third-best player in the NHL, behind only Wayne Gretzky and Mario Lemieux. This is the captain of the Red Wings, an All-Star, a skating wizard who is hockey's answer to the deer: graceful, elusive and smart.

He has 28 goals in the first 27 games this season, mountains of assists, his passing is deft, his aim is true, he is arguably the most popular athlete in Detroit — Yzerman, Isiah or Trammell, toss it up — and is certainly the most unanimously well-liked. The other night he went to a Stevie Wonder concert.

They could have called it: "Stevie Wonder meets Stevie Wonderful."

And he's embarrassed to say hello to Gordie Howe?

Oh, Yzerman. You'll never last.

And yet, well, who knows? Maybe we tapped into the real thing here — humility and talent in one handsome package. For years, Yzerman has been referred to as "Detroit's rising star." But he is the hottest scorer in hockey right now. He was recently NHL player of the month. He breaks a Gordie Howe record. Perhaps we should take a hint. Perhaps he has arrived for good.

Top of the heap — Gretzky, Lemieux, Yzerman.

Just don't tell him that.

"There's no comparison between Wayne Gretzky and me," Yzerman says, sitting in his West Bloomfield apartment, his voice, as always, soft and unassuming. "He's done it all. Won Stanley Cups, won scoring championships.... These people who compare us, or say he and Mario and I are 1-2-3, it's so unfair to guys like Mark Messier, Dale Hawerchuk, Ray Bourque. You can't compare. ...

"And Gordie Howe? No way. I was looking at some of his records the other day. He's got marks that will last forever. He played with a dynasty. If we ever become a dynasty, a lot of other guys will be breaking records, too."

He crosses his legs and folds his hands — and he looks as if he's 15 years old. Amazing. Most people see Yzerman only on the ice, when he's sweaty and his hair is wet and his sparse whiskers suggest at least a little ruggedness.

See him at home sometime. I bet he

gets carded at PG movies.

All of which makes his maturity a surprise. And know this: He is as mature as they come. Not just hockey-wise. Business-wise. Life-wise. And he's only 23.

You look at him and you say, "Geez, the guy belongs in high school." You listen to him, and you say, "Geez, the guy belongs in office."

Did you know that Steve Yzerman is studying to be a financial analyst? Yep. He's taking a course with Shearson Lehman Brothers.

"I don't want to be the typical dumb athlete," he says. "I mean, I'd like to have something to talk about other than hockey."

He also plans to be married, next year, to his longtime girlfriend, Lisa Brennan. They have a date all set. Now. I don't want to say he's passing up opportunities here. But if you put Steve Yzerman in a nightclub and told Detroit women he was there, we might never see him again.

"I know what I want from life," he says, shrugging, when asked about his adoring female fans. "Lisa was with me long before things got going good. And she'll be with me long after.

"Usually when we go out, I try to let it be known that I'm with her. Sometimes people will come over anyhow."

He laughs. "If I forget to introduce her, she kicks me in the shins."

Like most captains, Yzerman has learned to straddle the team's needs with the needs of the public. That is not surprising. What is surprising is that he learned it so fast. What can rattle Steve Yzerman now? When a horrible knee injury ended his regular season in March 1988, there were whispers; some said he would never be the same.

"I'll be back," he promised. And he delivered.

DETROIT ROYALTY: Red Wings greats Gordie Howe and Ted Lindsay present the Stanley Cup to Yzerman during a ceremony to kick off the 1997-98 season. The Stanley Cup win in 1997 was the club's first in 42 years — and the team would bring it back to Detroit again in 1998.
JULIAN H. GONZALEZ

During the recent escapades of Bob Probert and Petr Klima, he was not shy with criticism of his teammates. Nor did he play St. Steven in the media. "I think we've all talked enough about it," he said, when it seemed, indeed, we had.

Most athletes treat responsibility the way a vampire treats a cross. Yet in the four years I have known him, I have seen Yzerman agree to do one of those silly playoff "diaries" for our newspaper — then insist that he write it himself. I have seen him wandering around the Windsor airport parking lot in the wee hours of the morning, making sure his teammates all had rides home.

The other night on the radio, hockey analyst Don Cherry rated Yzerman up there with Gretzky and Lemieux in talent. "But you know," he added, "if you ask players around the league, Yzerman is the one they'd most like to sit and have beer with. He's the most regular guy of the three."

And then there is this story. I heard it from Mary Schroeder, a photographer for our newspaper, who sits near the penalty box at Joe Louis Arena. Whenever Yzerman gets called for a penalty, he enters the box, cursing like a sailor. Then he sees her.

"Sorry, Mary," he always says.

And he sits down.

Manners.

Now, OK. Before we put a halo around his head, let us point out that, yes, Yzerman is sometimes so low-key, he sounds like part of SCTV's "Great White North" bit. ("Have a sandwich, eh? OK, eh? Good, eh?") And he is not without his moods, his temper, his pet peeves. He is mortal. The knee injury still bothers him, he can't sprint without pain and squatting is pretty much out — it hurts too much.

But we are talking about a guy here who could become legendary. He could become (gulp) this era's Gordie Howe.

STANDING OVATION: Yzerman acknowledges a cheering Joe Louis Arena crowd after scoring his 600th goal against Edmonton in November 1999. Yzerman was the 11th NHL player to score 600, joining former Wings Gordie Howe and Marcel Dionne.

KIRTHMON F. DOZIER

STEVIE WONDERFUL

He is already the star on a team that is on the lip of excellence. And he is only 23. Detroit is a hockeytown. When the team goes good, the good are canonized.

And he is on his way. Quietly. Humbly.

His contract has become an issue lately because he earns only $385,000 annually, while Lemieux and Gretzky earn about $2 million. His response? It will be taken care of. Why debate it in the press?

"It seems like so many contracts become controversial. I don't see why they can't be harmonious, all parties getting along."

What planet did this guy come from?

And are there any more like him? I keep worrying that one day soon I'll walk into the Wings' locker room and Yzerman will be wearing sunglasses, flanked by a bodyguard and a personal secretary. "No time to talk today, babe," he'll say, checking his hair in the mirror. "Maybe next week."

Who knows? It could be that the Bobby Knights and Joaquin Andujars and Jim McMahons have ruined us. Maybe you get a humble guy who just wants to play and do well and marry his high school sweetheart, and you immediately grow suspicious.

Write something complimentary about an athlete these days. Next thing you know, the guy gets arrested.

But I don't think that will happen with Steve Yzerman. Call it a hunch. Call it blind faith.

There is now at least one part of the Red Wings' history book that reads:

1. Yzerman
2. Howe

And I suspect it won't be the last. Still, I could be wrong. "Are you comfortable with your image?" I ask.

"Um... I don't know what it is," he says.

I'm not wrong. Ⓖ

FILE PHOTO

AMONG THE GREATS: Yzerman's performance ranked him with the top players in the league, including Wayne Gretzky. "When you look at the Red Wings and see how Stevie and Chris Chelios help deflect the pressure of the situation from everyone else on the team, it makes it so much easier for the other guys," Gretzky said.

ADOPTED SON: Yzerman
was born in Canada, but
he became Detroit's
favorite son. He scored
his first goal in 1983 and
his last in 2006.
DAVID P. GILKEY

'A PURE RED WING'

"I'd like to stay in Detroit my entire career."
Yzerman, in 1988

On the eve of Yzerman's sixth season with the Red Wings, Free Press hockey writer Keith Gave wrote of The Captain:

BY KEITH GAVE

1988

OCTOBER 6

He is the winged wheel personified, an all-Canadian kid Detroiters have adopted as their own. He is the most famous hockey player in Detroit since Gordie Howe left town. If he does everything expected of him, his No. 19 will be raised to the rafters at Joe Louis Arena next to Howe's No. 9. Steve Yzerman is growing up before our very eyes.

Here's what Yzerman himself and some others were saying about The Captain.

General manager Jimmy Devellano, who calls Yzerman "a pure Red Wing" because he was drafted, developed and reached stardom in the organization: "Nothing would thrill me more than to have Steve Yzerman finish a 15-year career in Detroit. It's pure. It signifies something special in sports. I know it's the way Jack Adams (former Wings coach and general manager) used to feel about Gordie Howe. He's like a son. I feel a little sad when I think of Gordie Howe in Houston and Hartford" after spending 24 seasons in Detroit.

Yzerman: "I'd like to stay in Detroit my entire career. I don't know what's going to happen, whether they want me or not, but I know I don't want to go anywhere else. It's very rare, I know, but when you look at a lot of the greats in sports, they all played in one city... like (Jean) Beliveau and (Rocket) Richard in Montreal. I think you lose a little something when you move. You can always move for more money, but I don't believe in that. You see it a lot in baseball, which is why I admire Alan Trammell. He could go

FAN CLUB: With Yzerman on the ice, Detroit had plenty to cheer about. In a 2004 survey of Michigan registered voters, 15% named him Detroit's favorite sports hero of the past 20 years. Next was Barry Sanders with 10%.

KIRTHMON F. DOZIER

'A PURE RED WING'

a lot of other places and take the money, but he doesn't."

Yzerman, on being compared favorably with Trammell, the Tigers shortstop who was most valuable player in the 1984 World Series, and Isiah Thomas, the two-time NBA All-Star Game MVP who led the Pistons to the league championship final: "I really haven't done a whole lot to deserve it. Considering what I have done in my career and what Isiah and Alan have done, there's really no comparison. Our team has done well lately, but I still don't think I deserve it. I haven't done enough."

Devellano, recalling his decision to draft Yzerman: "Our scouting staff felt that any one of the three boys" — Pat LaFontaine, Sylvain Turgeon and Yzerman, all of whom were available after Brian Lawton was selected first — "were going to be pretty good and, in hindsight, we weren't too far off. But this was our first-ever draft as a management team, and it was so important that he be the right boy. And boy, oh boy, it's one of the nicest things that has happened to me since I've been in Detroit. He's been a shining light for us,

an absolute gem.... I really don't think I'd have made it without him, to be honest with you. He was just a great pick for our regime."

Darren Pang, former NHL goalie who grew up with Yzerman in the Ottawa suburb of Nepean: "He was very similar then (as a teenager) as he is now. He has a real sense of humor, kind of dry at times. He's kind of reserved, the kind of guy who doesn't make harsh judgments. Even at a young age, he was real mature. It seems like he always said and did the right things."

Pang again: "You can see why he's a

JULIAN H. GONZALEZ

LIVING LEGENDS: After announcing his retirement on July 3, 2006, Yzerman meets with Red Wings legend Gordie Howe. Yzerman said in 1988 that he would be embarrassed to approach Howe out of the blue to say hello. "I'll never reach that point," he said.

good captain. He's the ultimate leader. Sure, he's young and an exceptional player. But more than that, when he says something in the dressing room, everybody's going to listen to what he has to say. And in a pressure situation during the game, you know he's going to be there for you."

Jacques Demers on Yzerman's dark side: "You can always tell when he's having a bad day. He gets very quiet. He won't say a word to anybody. I just leave him alone then."

Lisa Brennan, Yzerman's wife-to-be: "He's got a pretty bad temper. He doesn't explode too often, but when he does. ... It's usually when he can't fix something. He's such a perfectionist. He has to do everything himself."

Yzerman, on what he might be doing if not for his mastery of hockey: "I'd probably be finishing high school (ha-ha). I'm not sure, really. I'd probably still be in university, or just graduated. I know it's not good advice to kids, but all I ever thought about was playing hockey. School took a backseat when I started moving up. I just played hockey. I did what I had to do, nothing else."

Yzerman on fame and fortune: "Well, fortune hasn't affected me a whole lot because I don't have one yet. But I'm working on that." As for the fame: "It was nice just being a hockey player before, with people knowing who you are. Now I still enjoy it, but I'm a little more reserved. I like to stay to myself. I'm a little more private.

"When I was a kid, I used to think that hockey players were like God or something. I thought it would be great to be a hero like that. Then I got there and it's no big deal. It's really no different than playing midget or peewee. It's still just playing the game. Sure, you want to make money, but the guys here are still out there trying hard and playing to win. It's not for the bonuses. It's just winning. You get happy or frustrated just like we did when we were kids."

Yzerman on fatherhood: "Oh, I don't know about that. I think we'll try a dog first and see how that goes." ⏻

FAMILY MAN: Yzerman holds daughter Isabella as he and his wife, Lisa, are introduced before a 1996 game against the Chicago Blackhawks. The Yzermans have been married since 1989 and have three daughters, Isabella, Maria and Sophia.

MARY SCHROEDER

BOYS' NIGHT OUT

We were going to a baseball game, Joe Dumars, Barry Sanders, Steve Yzerman and me.

BY MITCH ALBOM

1990

SEPTEMBER 13

It was two hours before the first pitch when Joe Dumars jumped in the car. He was late. He apologized. He stretched his long legs in the backseat and grinned like a kid.

"I hope Cecil hits one tonight," he said.

"Yeah," I said.

"And no singles or anything."

"Nuh-uh."

"I mean, it's like singles don't count with Cecil, you know?"

"Uh-huh."

"Got to be a home run."

"Yep."

A pause. "Preferably a long home run."

"A long home run," I repeated.

"Yeah," said Joe, leaning back.

We were going to a baseball game, Joe Dumars, Barry Sanders, Steve Yzerman and me. I had the tickets, which might be the only reason I got in the group. Then again, it's a pretty nice group. Considering these are the reigning superstars in basketball, football and hockey in this town, their egos are in nice perspective. You buy them a hot dog, they say, "Hey, thanks a lot."

They meet Sparky Anderson, they act like impressed fans. A foul ball comes their way and they.... But I'm getting ahead of myself.

"What's Barry doing?" Joe asked as the car sped along Long Lake Road.

"He's got practice today," I said.

Dumars looked at the car clock. It read 5:30. "This long?" he said.

I nodded.

"Man," he said, "football is really a job, isn't it?"

We pulled into the Silverdome parking lot. There was Barry Sanders, standing alone by his car. Hands in his pockets. Nobody around. This, remember, is

DETROIT'S FINEST: The leading men of Detroit sports meet for a game at Tiger Stadium in 1999: from left, Barry Sanders of the Lions, Cecil Fielder of the Tigers, Steve Yzerman and Joe Dumars of the Pistons.

MARY SCHROEDER

> Of course, it wouldn't be a game without hot dogs, and so I yelled for the vendor. "Four!" He passed them down, from Yzerman to Sanders to Dumars to me.

JULIAN H. GONZALEZ

TOP OF THEIR GAME: When Cecil Fielder met Steve Yzerman at Tiger Stadium in 1999, Fielder was leading the league in homers. That same year, Yzerman led the Wings in points (74) and in power-play goals (13).

arguably the best running back in the NFL, the rookie who needed 10 yards in the final game to win the NFC rushing title last season and told his coach, "Don't bother to put me back in. Just let's win and go home."

He shyly opened the door and slid inside, dressed in shorts and a pink T-shirt. "Hey, man," he said to Dumars. "Hey, man," he said to me.

"Thanks for coming," I said.

"No problem," he said.

"Should be fun," Joe said. "Cecil might hit one."

Barry smiled and nodded. The car pulled away. About 10 seconds later, Barry leaned in. He looked troubled.

"Um, to be honest," he said, "I don't really know who Cecil Fielder is."

One thing you will quickly learn about superstar athletes: They are not all alike. Take Dumars and Sanders, for example. Dumars can watch a baseball game on TV from beginning to end. He can watch volleyball. He can stare at ESPN while using the Stairmaster and absorb everything.

And then there is Sanders, who has never seen a Tigers game on TV. In fact, he has been to only one other baseball game in his life. "I don't have the time," he says, almost embarrassed.

But then, out of the blue, he turns to Dumars and says, "I was a pretty good basketball player, though."

Dumars smiles. "You were?"

"I played three years varsity in high school."

"So you were better than me."

"Well... yeah, I guess I was."

And Dumars exploded in laughter. And so did Sanders. And from that point on, they were like pals. They chatted the whole ride down, about training, about mutual friends. At one point, Sanders gave Dumars his phone number and asked if maybe they could get together, hang around.

And here came the ballpark.

"We're meeting Yzerman here," I said. I looked at Barry. He had that same puzzled look.

"Steve Yzerman?" I said. "The Red Wings' captain?"

Well. Anyhow. There was Steve, right on time, and everyone shook hands, we all took the tickets and we walked toward the field. Tiger Stadium smelled of sausages and peanuts and greasepaint. "Nothing like a ball-park," said Dumars, sniffing. Yzerman waved at a fan. Sanders just looked around.

And then we were on the field. And there was Cecil Fielder, signing autographs. Sanders tugged on my sleeve. "That's him, right, No. 45?"

"Fielder," I said. "Leads the league in home runs."

Sanders nodded. "He's big."

Which is a compliment, I guess, coming from a football player.

Anyhow, I approached Cecil, mostly because the other guys were too shy to do it. And here was the moment I had waited for:

Fielder. Sanders. Dumars. Yzerman.

Talk about your basic elements. It's was like Hydrogen meeting Oxygen.

"My MAN!" said Fielder, throwing an arm around Dumars. "Aw, man, this guy can hoop!"

"My MAN!" he continued, throwing an arm around Sanders. "Aw, man, this guy can scoot with the football."

"My MAN!" he continued, grabbing Yzerman's hand. "Uh, nice to meet you."

I don't think hockey is Cecil's big sport.

Anyhow, pretty soon it was like one big party. Cecil gave everyone a bat with his number on it. "Take some batting practice!" he insisted, pointing to the cage. They all just grinned and shuffled their feet.

Did I mention Sparky Anderson? Oh, yeah. He snuck up and grabbed Dumars from behind and slapped his back. And he shook hands with Yzerman and Sanders. Barry had that awkward smile on his face again, so I slid up alongside him.

"Sparky Anderson," I whispered.

"Yeah," he mumbled, "I've seen him on the commercials. He's pretty famous, isn't he?"

And soon, we were heading for our seats. Barry. Steve. Joe. A couple people oohed and aahed and a couple kids wanted autographs, but mostly we were left alone and we stood for the national anthem. I asked Yzerman if he'd ever caught a foul ball at a baseball game.

"I never even came close," he said. "I sat on the third-base side a whole game and never even saw one."

Not long after that, the Yankees' batter fouled off a pitch and it lofted high in the air. For a moment, it was headed our way but then it drifted toward the third-base side, and a brown-haired young man caught it with his bare hands.

"Hey!" Yzerman yelled to me suddenly. "You know who caught that?"

"Who?" I asked.

"Tim Cheveldae."

I looked at the front row. Damn if he wasn't right.

Goalies get to catch everything.

Anyhow, the game went on and finally Cecil came to the plate. I'd like to say he hit a home run in that first at-bat. He didn't. Actually, he struck out. But that didn't seem to dampen anyone's spirit.

Of course, it wouldn't be a game without hot dogs, and so I yelled for the vendor. "Four!" He passed them down, from Yzerman to Sanders to Dumars to me. And I passed him the money, me to Dumars to Sanders to Yzerman. And when Yzerman leaned over to hand me the change, he reached in front of Sanders. And he turned and said, "Excuse me."

And then Sanders reached around and said, "Thanks for the hot dog, man."

I thought that was nice.

Everyone had to get home early, and pretty soon it was time to go. Steve said good-bye and drove himself back to Grosse Pointe, as unassuming as ever. And Sanders and Dumars could have gone home separately, but they talked it

AN AVERAGE DAY? Barry Sanders, pictured, joined Joe Dumars, Steve Yzerman and Mitch Albom at a Tigers game.

over and decided to go together. I walked them out, we shook hands. And they thanked me several times. The game was still going on inside.

Earlier in the day, when the arrangements for this little idea were getting confused, my boss said, "God, why did we ever try this?" But you know what? It turned out OK. Barry. Steve. Joe. It wasn't three big egos trying to outdo one another. It wasn't three superstars who demanded luxury-box treatment.

It was basically three guys at the ballpark on a late-summer night with a few hot dogs and a few Cokes and some unusual conversation. You couldn't do this in every city. Detroit is awful lucky that the biggest guys in town are also the nicest and most unassuming.

I thought maybe that was the lesson of the evening. And just as I picked up the phone to send this story, in the bottom of the ninth, with Joe and Barry and Steve maybe listening on the car radio, Cecil Fielder stepped to the plate and whacked a 2-1 fastball that hit the leftfield roof of Tiger Stadium. Home run No. 46.

You know what I figure? I figure it's a perfect ending. That's what I figure. ●

THE END OF THE BEGINNING

BY KEITH GAVE

1993
MAY 2

The Red Wings bowed out of the 1993 playoffs with a numbing, Game 7 overtime loss to underdog Toronto.

After a sleepless night spent second-guessing himself and worrying about his heartbroken players, the general manager of the Red Wings arose facing more questions than answers.

Bryan Murray was chugging coffee, his season over and quite likely, he said, his coaching career, too. So instead of preparing his team to play St. Louis in the second round, Murray was left to contemplate an uncertain future.

But the past is prologue. His reputation as a coach whose teams always found a way to lose in the playoffs was now his indelible legacy. This was to be the year he finally would exorcise those demons. This was the team, with no apparent weakness, that he would ride to the finals. This would be his swan song.

Instead, he is left to deal with the devastation of a first-round playoff knockout that followed a record-setting regular season. He expects no sympathy for himself, but wishes it for his players.

"I've been lucky. I've had lots of chances," he said. "I wanted it for this group of players. It's tough for some of them to accept. They deserved better."

Now, rather than coach his team, Murray must reconstruct it, starting with the shattered egos of some of his most important players. Captain Steve Yzerman faces a long summer of self-doubt after his finest season ended with another playoff disappointment.

STEVIE, SUBDUED: After a grueling Game 7 overtime loss to Toronto in 1993, Yzerman takes his turn to discuss what went wrong. The team was knocked out of the playoffs in the first round after a record-setting regular season.

JULIAN H. GONZALEZ

BEAM US A CUP, SCOTTY
THE AGONY ... AND THE ECSTASY
DREAM ON
FIRST BRUSH WITH STANLEY
ZINGING THE BLUES
MILE-HIGH LOW

CLOSE BUT NO CIGAR

BEAM US A CUP, SCOTTY

WINNING MOVE: "I think it is time to win the Stanley Cup, and Scotty Bowman will give us our best opportunity," Red Wings owner Mike Ilitch said after naming Bowman head coach.

"I think it's time to win the Stanley Cup, and Scotty Bowman will give us our best opportunity," Red Wings owner Mike Ilitch said.

BY KEITH GAVE

1993
JUNE 15

And with that, a self-described sore loser put the exclamation point on perhaps the most anticlimactic story of the spring: Scotty Bowman finally was named as the Red Wings' new coach. What's news is Ilitch's sudden assertiveness. As he did in his first conversation with Bowman, Ilitch spoke like a man willing to do anything to win, including becoming more demanding of the players he has babied for too long.

"We've got to put more emphasis on winning," Ilitch said. "I've tiptoed in sports a little bit. Maybe I should say what I've felt more often."

Ilitch let his actions do his talking for him, hiring the six-time Stanley Cup champion.

"The one thing that stuck in my mind was when Mike Ilitch said to me, 'We've owned the team for 11 years, and we've never won the Stanley Cup. We're not proud of that fact,' " Bowman said. "He said, 'We're not great losers here. These 11 years without a Cup are really starting to bother me.'

"That certainly triggered in my mind that that's what Mike and Marian Ilitch want so badly for the city of Detroit. They want to win. I know that. The players should know it, too. Now it's time to go do it....

"These players are treated very well. It's a great place to play, and they'll be expected to win." ☉

> **"We've got to put more emphasis on winning."**
> Mike Ilitch, Wings owner

THE AGONY ... AND THE ECSTASY

Yzerman finished the 1993-94 season with 24 goals among 82 points and with a happy addition to his family.

BY KEITH GAVE

After missing 26 games with a herniated disk in his upper back, Steve Yzerman scored a goal and an assist in his first game back for new coach Scotty Bowman. He finished the 1993-94 season with 24 goals among 82 points.

Yzerman returned to the lineup one game and four days ahead of schedule. Patience was never one of his strong suits, and he decided 67 days of inactivity during the season was enough. Both he and the Wings had said for weeks that New Year's Eve was his target date for returning.

Yzerman said he expected to play his normal game.

"I went my whole career trying to avoid being hit, so I'm not looking to start now," he said. "But I expect to get bumped a little bit. I'm just looking forward to coming back. It's easy right now because the team's playing great."

◆ ◆ ◆

The way Steve Yzerman made a beeline for the net after scoring his 17th goal of the season, it was obvious it meant something special. When the Wings' newest father left the hospital before the game, wife Lisa told him to score a goal for his daughter, Isabella Katharine, who was born Feb. 22, 1994.

And he did.

"I'm going to keep it," Yzerman said. Isabella is the couple's first child. ◗

CARRY ON: Yzerman missed 26 games early in the 1993-94 season because of a herniated disk before returning to play for new coach Scotty Bowman.
KIRTHMON F. DOZIER

JULIAN H. GONZALEZ

STILL WAITING: The grand prize eluded the Red Wings in 1994 and again in 1995, when they watched the New Jersey Devils hoist the Stanley Cup.

BY MITCH ALBOM

1994
APRIL 30

This story was written a day before the Red Wings were eliminated — for the second straight season — in the first round of the playoffs.

Steve Yzerman looks like hell. Or as much as a heartthrob can look like hell. The left side of his face has a red mark from forehead to chin — "a glove cut," he says — and his pouty upper lip still has the vertical scar

from 30 stitches, turning it purple and slightly swollen. His knees are both in the danger zone, one from an old injury and one from the newest injury, suffered two weeks ago — the one the Wings are so hush-hush about, but which, I can tell you, is the medial ligament of what used to be his "good" knee — and, given its severity, most people wouldn't even think jogging, let alone hockey.

Yzerman is not most people. He has

spare tanks of courage and a shrinking supply of patience. He's been playing this game professionally for 10 years, has been one of its superstars, certainly as much as a Charles Barkley or Patrick Ewing has been an NBA superstar, and yet, every spring, here he is, in a fight for his playoff life — just to get out of the first round.

"I was thinking the other day about 1987, when we went to the semifinals against Edmonton," Yzerman says, sitting in a sweatshirt and a baseball cap after practice. "I look around this room and there are so few guys left. There's Shawn Burr, Probie (Bob Probert), Steve Chiasson and me.

"But the thing I remember most is that we were playing one night, and we were the only game you could watch on TV. America or Canada. Only four teams were left in the playoffs, and that night was our game. All of hockey was watching us.

"That was such a great feeling."

He looks down, perhaps realizing that the highlight of his career was a semifinal that ended in defeat. And any sports fan has to feel for the guy.

Steve Yzerman doesn't need my sympathy, yours either, but talk to him for a while and you find yourself wanting to help, the way you help a bright kid who needs a college scholarship, or an innocent motorist broken down on the highway.

Yzerman, too, seems stranded on the highway. For much of his career, he was lumped with Wayne Gretzky and Mario Lemieux as the league's top three players. But Gretzky and Lemieux have tasted champagne from the Stanley Cup, more than once. Meanwhile, Yzerman, about to turn 29, says, "They can retire because they've already accomplished what they want. I'm still chasing my dream."

Here's my theory: Your dreams keep you young. Yzerman's dreams remain unfulfilled, hockey-wise, so he keeps pushing back the end of his rainbow.

And he keeps fighting to get there. You knew the guy would drag himself back from this most-recent injury, the way he's dragged himself back so many times before. And he'll be out there, with the "C" on his sweater, trying yet again to push Detroit hockey into May.

Still, all these early exits during his prime years have torn away at his insides. In 1993, after the first-round loss to Toronto and the return of the nagging trade rumors, something snapped.

"I just decided the hell with all this worrying that I'll never get my chance. I can't do it anymore. It's so tiring. I decided I'll try to be a good player, a good person, and good things should happen. I tell myself I have lots of hockey left. That's how I live with it." Ⓒ

JULIAN H. GONZALEZ

SHOW OF SUPPORT: Wings fans, who stood behind their team through thick and thin, also would have to wait for happier times.

BYE-BYE, BRYAN

On June 1, 1994, Red Wings general manager Bryan Murray made it official: Captain Steve Yzerman is on the trading block.

"I will talk about him now," Murray said of trade discussions with other clubs. "We have to see what Steve Yzerman might bring in the market."

 Murray said Yzerman's name hasn't surfaced in serious trade talks in three years — since the Wings tried to acquire Pat LaFontaine from the New York Islanders. A possible trade was discussed when Yzerman met with Murray shortly after another disappointing playoff season.

"I asked Steve about that," Murray said. "He, like a lot of our key guys, feels that a change or two among the core group of guys is probably necessary. He said, 'I'm not sure, Bryan, what's best for me or what's best for the team. I'd just like to get the job done here.'

"But Steve Yzerman would not be shocked if I went to him and said, 'Steve, I'm going to try to move you to another team.' He understands we have to think about everybody now."

Two days later, Bryan Murray was fired.

FIRST BRUSH WITH STANLEY

"I can't believe we're finally going."
Yzerman, upon advancing to the Cup finals, the team's first since 1966

BY MITCH ALBOM

1995
JUNE 12

An hour after the game — after the Red Wings eliminated Chicago and advanced to their first Stanley Cup finals in 29 years — Steve Yzerman sat inside the locker room in a happy daze, still wearing his sweat-soaked red undershirt and pushing his wet hair from his forehead as he said, "We're finally going.... I can't believe we're finally going."

The nicest moment of Detroit's heart-thumping, 2-1, double-overtime win was not the last goal or the flying octopi or even Bruce Martyn yelling, "He scoooo-res!"

The nicest moment was when Yzerman hugged Shawn Burr, his long-time teammate, then lifted that Campbell bowl and shook it over his head and heard the applause rain down like confetti.

"I didn't know what you do with the trophy," Yzerman admitted. "Do you take a lap with it or what? I was a little embarrassed. Finally I looked at (Paul) Coffey and he said, 'Let's get outta here.' I've never had a moment like that. I never heard it that loud. It was so loud."

Sweat dripped off Yzerman's chin. A bandage was on his right knee, on which he had surgery two weeks earlier. At one point during the game, he was knocked down, got up, skated gingerly to the bench and went straight into the locker room. Fans thought he was done, injured, finished. But he came back 10 minutes later and was on the ice — and next thing you knew, he scored the tying goal.

"A minor problem," Yzerman said afterward, waving it off. Of course, a minor problem for Yzerman is brain surgery to everyone else. If anyone thinks this guy is not the fiercest inspiration inside the Detroit locker room, think again. Players respond more to courage than to statistics, and they have seen a wounded Yzerman make more comebacks than a dog's bone. It is the reason he is the leader of this team.

"When Stevie grabbed me at center ice, he said something like, 'Burrsie, all those years of nothing and now this!' " 🅖

TRYING TIME: Yzerman's first trip to the Stanley Cup finals was disappointing; the New Jersey Devils swept the Red Wings.

MARY SCHROEDER

OH, HELL

From glory to gory in one week. What a stunning turnaround for the Red Wings, such a dominant team through the regular season and playoffs. They made it to the Stanley Cup finals but will spend the rest of the summer trying to live down their performance once they got there.

When it was over, when the New Jersey Devils had completed their four-game sweep to the Cup, the Wings were numb.

They were in tears.

They were in shock.

"That's the emotional roller coaster of sports," defenseman Paul Coffey said. "One day you're on top, the next day you feel like crap. A lot of good things happened this year. Unfortunately, the big thing didn't happen, which was our ultimate goal. We set out to win the Stanley Cup, from that point we fell short."

- Viv Bernstein

ZINGING THE BLUES

"It's the kind of goal every player dreams about in his career. Including me." Yzerman, on his Game 7 gem

In the 1996 playoffs, Yzerman scored what many consider to be the biggest goal of his career.

BY MITCH ALBOM

1996

MAY 16

It was every suspense film you ever watched, every thriller you ever read, every nervous waiting room you ever sat in all rolled into one nail-biting, double-overtime evening at Joe Louis Arena, 19,000 exhausted fans, tapping their chests at every break to make sure the old ticker was still working.

And finally, a few minutes before midnight, the doctor emerged, smiling with the good news:

It's a goal!

"YES! YES! YES!" the fans screamed, when Steve Yzerman put an end to the most dramatic playoff game here in years, whacking a 55-foot shot past the seemingly impenetrable Jon Casey to win Game 7 of this second-round series, 1-0. The crowd erupted like an uncorked volcano, and Yzerman himself was actually lifted into the air by the force of his own exuberance, running and cheering as his skates never touched the ice.

It's a goal!

Breathe again.

"I don't usually score that way," Yzerman said, sheepishly, after the goal that ended this agonizing series, one in which the Wings blew a lead, nearly fell off the cliff and fought back to take the final two games. "It's the kind of goal every player dreams about in his career. Including me."

"Had you ever scored in double-overtime before?" he was asked.

"Never," he said.

"Did you get the puck?"

He smiled. "I got the puck."

Well. How could he not? What a finish! What a perfect end! A night that desperately called for a hero got the call from the perfect cast member, The Captain himself, a guy who has been waiting for this night longer than anyone on the roster, and has been playing recently as if the last lights of his life hung in the scoreboard. Even the opposing coach, Mike Keenan, called him "the best player in the series." And just seconds before his miracle goal, he'd set up a perfect chance for teammate Sergei Fedorov, putting the puck in front of the net. But Fedorov slapped it into Casey and was denied, as were 38 shots before his.

Yzerman figured "do it yourself."

A few seconds later, he did, whacking a high, stinging shot that hit the crossbar with a "ping" and fell in behind a startled Casey.

It's a goal!

Breathe again.

The Blues are history now. There is a team from Colorado to deal with. But before we move onto that series, remember the words of Yzerman, the captain, before Game 7. He encouraged the fans — as well as his teammates — to keep in mind this is a sport, and to "relax and have fun."

Once we start breathing again, we can do that.

"What were you thinking the moment you saw that red light go on?" Yzerman was asked.

"Honestly?" he answered. "I thought, 'It went in? No way!' "

Way. Ⓖ

HERO: Steve Yzerman skates off the ice after hitting a 55-foot shot to end a nerve-wracking, double overtime Game 7 in the second round of the 1996 playoffs.

FILE PHOTO

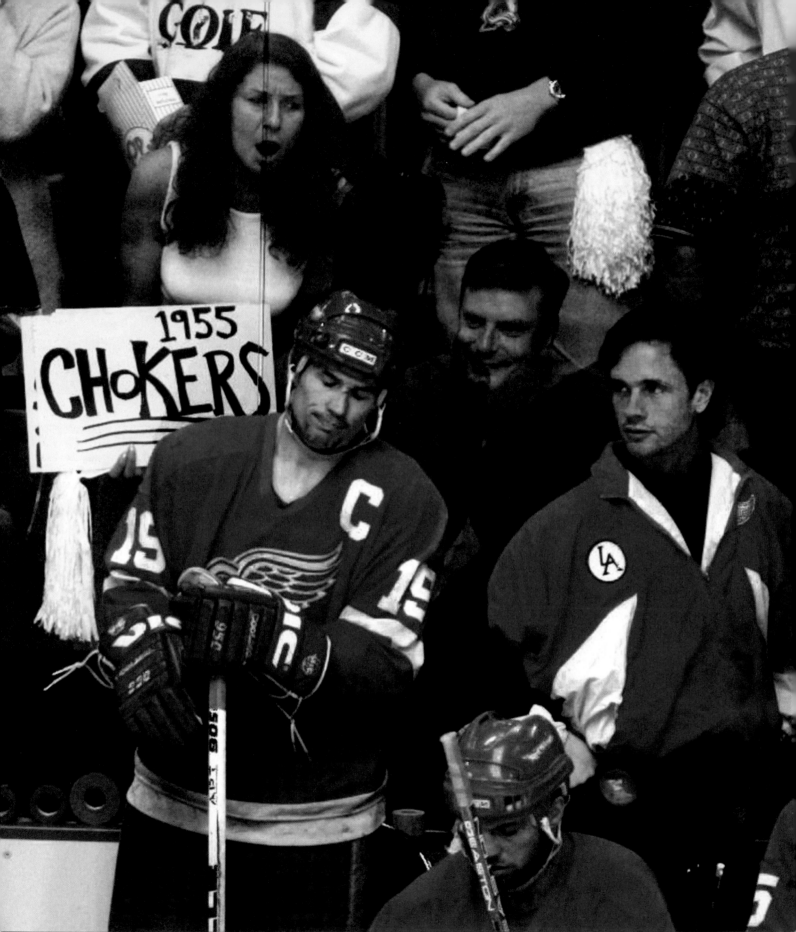

JULIAN H. GONZALEZ

SIGN OF THE TIMES: Disappointment is etched in Yzerman's face as the Red Wings come up short in Colorado.

MILE-HIGH LOW

"It's like getting your heart torn out."

Darren McCarty, after Colorado eliminated the Wings from the playoffs in 1996

BY MITCH ALBOM

1996

MAY 29

DENVER — The dream died in the mountains, a mile above sea level, where the air is thin and it is difficult to breathe.

And as cold reality sank in — one goal behind, two goals behind, three goals behind — you could feel the Red Wings players gasping, suffocating, all the good things they had done this season crashing to earth like a boulder during an avalanche. Or should we say Avalanche?

Snowed under.

See ya next dream.

This one is over, a carcass to be picked apart by the second-guessers, food for the talk shows, grist for the mill. And when all the talk is done, you will still know nothing more than this: The Wings saved their worst for last, played their most inconsistent hockey of the year during the Stanley Cup playoffs, and continued a mystifying tradition of running out of gas when the prize is within reach.

Perhaps the most symbolic moment came when young Kris Draper, who had embodied so much of the fresh-faced hope of this team, was blindsided into the wall by Colorado's master villain, Claude Lemieux. When Draper finally got up, his face was buried in a towel, so he could not see, several teeth had been knocked out, so he could not smile, and he left the ice, so he could not play. The maintenance crew ran out and shoveled up his bloody ice, tossing it in a wastebasket.

Snowed under.

"It's like getting your heart torn out," said a dejected Darren McCarty after the 4-1 loss to Colorado ended the Wings' season in the Western Conference finals — one round short of the finals they achieved last year. "It hurts the Wings and everyone in the Red Wings' family, but we have to live with it because we're responsible."

Where's the justice in this, Wings fans ask?

The oldest curse in hockey loses to the newest town in the league. And instead of the pictures Detroit fans hoped to frame, we get snapshots of disaster, unimaginable just a few weeks ago. Instead of Chris Osgood plucking a save, we get cocky Patrick Roy, scooping the Wings shots and raising them over his head like a matador's cape. Instead of No. 19 of the Red Wings, Steve Yzerman, shaking a conference trophy over his head, we get No. 19 of the Avalanche, Joe Sakic, having his coming-out party in these playoffs, scoring twice, assisting on another goal, and doing the victory dance himself.

In fact, the only thing familiar is defeat. That, Wings fans have seen before. Forty-one years without winning a Stanley Cup. Still the longest wait in the National Hockey League. And as the final seconds ticked away, you could almost see the cursed ghosts descend like dead weight on the shoulders of the Wings, driving their skates deep into the ice, slowing them to a halt, and finally, a surrender.

Blue light. Game over.

See ya next dream. ☉

AVALANCHE: Colorado's Claude Lemieux blindsides the Wings' Kris Draper into the wall. Draper left the game with a bloody face while his teammates left with bruised egos.

ASSOCIATED PRESS

GLORY
YEARS

THOUGHTS OF HOME
BELIEVE!
MVP
FOLLOW THE LEADER
CAN'T WIN 'EM ALL
GOLDEN BOY
'C' IS FOR CHARACTER
HANG 10

SMELL THE ROSES

"We got a good hockey team, and we're going to win a lot of games."
Yzerman, on the eve of the 1996-97 season

BY KEITH GAVE

Many good things happened to the Red Wings during the 1995-96 season.

Steve Yzerman scored his 500th goal.

Paul Coffey became the first defenseman in the history of the league to reach 1,000 assists.

Dino Ciccarelli scored goal No. 545 and passed Maurice Richard on the all-time list.

Scotty Bowman's team broke an NHL record with 62 wins in an 82-game season.

Then along came Colorado, and the Avalanche buried Detroit's dream of a Stanley Cup parade. We all suffered the worst kind of disappointment. And we were angry.

"It's all our own fault — nobody else's but the players'," Coffey said on the eve of the 1996-97 season.

"But we learn by our mistakes.... We've got to stop and smell the roses along the way a little bit more.... We have such a great bunch of guys, and our young guys are so full

of fire. And everybody's goal in this room is to win the Stanley Cup."

Yzerman, who endured so many lean seasons before the Wings became a regular-season dynasty, said:

"This year, if something good happens, we should enjoy the moment more so and be proud of it. We can't worry about what happened in last year's playoffs or the playoffs before that. We've got to be proud of what we've accomplished but realize there's more to do. We shouldn't feel ashamed about anything.

"We've got a good hockey team, and we're going to win a lot of games. Let's enjoy it because the playoff run is really, well, I think everybody has gotten to realize how up-and-down it is, what an emotional experience it is and how draining it can be. I just don't like to look that far ahead this time of year. The playoffs are there, and we'll deal with that when we get there." ☺

JULIAN H. GONZALEZ

NOT BAD, BOYS: The Wings' 1995-96 regular season had its share of highlights, including Yzerman's 500th career goal and Detroit's NHL-record 62 wins in an 82-game season. But then came the playoffs, where the Avs took six games to beat the Wings in the Western Conference finals.

AV-VENGED

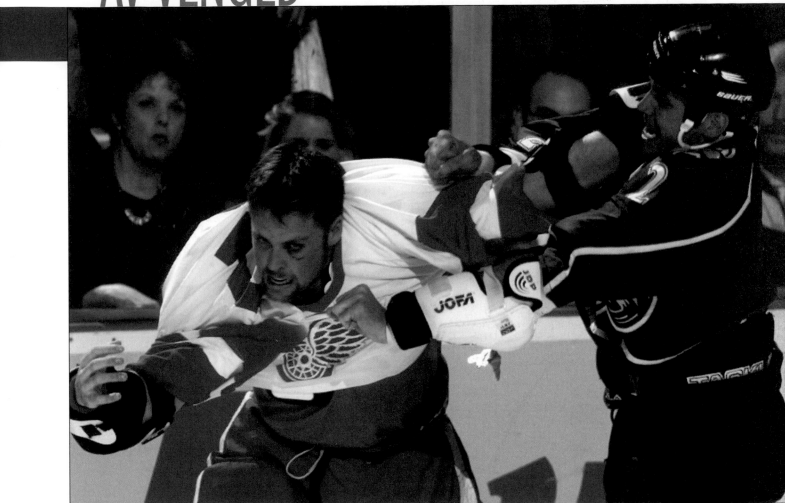

DAVID P. GILKEY

NO LOVE LOST: Detroit and Colorado had been squabbling for years, but in the 1997 playoffs, Aaron Ward and the Red Wings finally got the upper hand.

A city's hopes are renewed. The impossible seems possible again — the Red Wings' winning the Stanley Cup. A 42-year dream is four victories away.

BY JASON LA CANFORA

1997
MAY 26

Picture Steve Yzerman's name inscribed inches from Gordie Howe's. Mike Vernon's near Terry Sawchuk's. Vladimir Konstantinov's by Red Kelly's. The 1955 Detroit Red Wings and the 1997 Wings gracing the most sought-after trophy in professional sports.

It could happen.

The Wings advanced to the finals for the second time in three years by eliminating defending champion Colorado, 3-1, in Game 6 of the Western Conference finals at Joe Louis Arena. The Wings will face Eastern Conference champion Philadelphia in the finals.

"We all know that finishing second in the Stanley Cup finals means absolutely nothing," said Yzerman, the Wings captain for 11 seasons. "You sit and watch every year, and you get to know a lot of guys, and you see them winning and envy is the exact word. I'm excited about the opportunity to try again."

The Wings have won seven Stanley Cups, the most of any U.S.-based team. They are making their 20th appearance in the finals and first since they were swept by New Jersey in 1995.

By beating the Avs, the Wings avenged last spring's loss to Colorado in the conference finals.

"They did to us what we did to them last year," Avalanche captain Joe Sakic said. "They were hungrier than we were."

The arch-nemesis was a threat no longer. Claude Lemieux, who refused to shake Darren McCarty's hand during postgame ceremonies, is history, as is the Avalanche. This is Mike Vernon's time, Igor Larionov's time, Steve Yzerman's time.

"I was the drafted the same year as Stevie, and we went through a lot of tough times together in the late '80s," Joe Kocur said. "I can't put into words how special it would be to see him win a Cup."

It could happen. **G**

> **"They did to us what we did to them last year."**
> Joe Sakic, Avs captain

ONE WIN AWAY

THE 1995-96

DETROIT RED WINGS 1996-97

MIKE ILITCH   MARIAN ILITCH   ATANAS ILITCH
CHRISTOPHER ILITCH   DENISE ILITCH LITES   RONALD ILITCH
MICHAEL ILITCH   LISA ILITCH   MURRAY CAROLE ILITCH TREPECK
JIM DEVELLANO   SCOTTY BOWMAN   KEN HOLLAND   BARRY SMITH
DAVE LEWIS   MIKE KRUSHELNYSKI   JIM NILL   DAN BELISLE
MARK HOWE   HAKAN ANDERSSON   JOHN WHARTON
PAUL BOYER   TIM ABBOTT   SERGEI MNATSAKANOV

STEVE YZERMAN   DOUG BROWN   MATHIEU DANDENAULT   KRIS DRAPER
SERGEI FEDOROV   VIACHESLAV FETISOV   KEVIN HODSON
TOMAS HOLMSTROM   JOE KOCUR   VLADIMIR KONSTANTINOV
VYACHESLAV KOZLOV   MARTIN LAPOINTE   IGOR LARIONOV
NICKLAS LIDSTROM   KIRK MALTBY   DARREN McCARTY   LARRY MURPHY
CHRIS OSGOOD   JAMIE PUSHOR   BOB ROUSE   TOMAS SANDSTROM
BRENDAN SHANAHAN   TIM TAYLOR   MIKE VERNON   AARON WARD

ANDREW JOHNSTON

LEAVING A MARK: After winning the first three games of the finals against the Flyers, the Wings were on the brink of seeing their names becoming a permanent fixture on the Stanley Cup.

His wife says he comes home and looks right through her. Sits at the table. Sits on the couch. Looks right through her. Oh, he's pleasant enough.

BY MITCH ALBOM

1997
JUNE 6

He'll chat about the kid, the house — never hockey — but he's not really there. His eyes are locked on something off in the distance. In that way, I guess, Steve Yzerman is like a lot of working men. He doesn't want to talk about it.

But what he can't put into words these days is not frustration or embarrassment, although, like most of us, he has had plenty of those. No, what's perplexing Yzerman is this coming tidal wave of happiness. He hears it rumbling toward our city, he sees it on the horizon. He asks himself, "What should I do now?"

This is what he does. He goes within himself. He stops reading newspapers and stops listening to radio and TV and he furrows his brow and he says very little because the fight is not over, not yet, not yet, and so, in typical fashion, the man Detroit calls The Captain chooses quiet as his ally.

Quiet will be his friend. He will skate with the quiet in Game 4 of the Stanley Cup finals, calming himself, telling himself as the noise rains down that it is just another hockey game, just another night to lose a bucket of sweat and do whatever it takes to win.

And his heart will be going a million miles an hour.

There was a moment before Game 3 of these Stanley Cup finals against Philadelphia, when the Wings were introduced and the sellout crowd at Joe Louis Arena lost control. It was when Yzerman's name was called.

The noise was deafening, it rattled the roof and cascaded down to the ice. Even the announcer had to wait before he could be heard over the loudspeaker system.

"I really wasn't expecting anything like that," Yzerman said. "The only way I can describe it is if you have children, and you've been away for a while, and you come home and the dog is barking and the kids run at you and they're all excited."

"Like coming home?" I said.

"Yeah, it was like coming home," he said.

Last season, his name was trade bait. Remember? Rumors had him emptying his locker. And then he skated onto the Joe Louis ice for the first home game, and the crowd gave him such a deep, long, noisy ovation that anyone even thinking of trading him would have to join the Witness Protection Program.

Yzerman became a Red Wing for life that night.

If the Wings win the Cup, he could become one for the ages.

"Are you doing anything to record this past week?" I asked. "Are you taping the games, making a scrapbook, anything like that?"

He shook his head no, as if he hadn't even thought about it. "Right now, all I want to do is prepare. I don't want to let my guard down."

But the tidal wave is coming, and so is his release. Should the Wings win, there will be no need for the safe side of Yzerman's emotions. No reason to embrace the quiet. This is the end of the long, lonely wait.

And that mysterious rumble that Yzerman hears is his destiny, rolling in. If the horn sounds happily, it would only be fitting that No. 19 start the party, raise the Cup, throw back his head and let loose a holler that's been a long, marvelous career in the making.

After all, he is The Captain.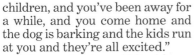

FALL GUY: Philadelphia's Paul Coffey is victimized by former teammates Brendan Shanahan, left, and Martin Lapointe during Detroit's Game 2 win in the Cup finals.

MARY SCHROEDER

DREAM COME TRUE

"I don't know how to describe the way I feel. I'm glad the game is over, but I wished it never ended." Yzerman, after winning the Stanley Cup

BY JASON LA CANFORA
AND MITCH ALBOM

1997
JUNE 7

The future Hall of Famer emerged from Joe Louis Arena about 3:15 in the morning carrying the one thing he had waited all his life to earn. Steve Yzerman, the Red Wings' captain for 11 years, strutted out of the dressing room with the Stanley Cup held above his head, walked into the players' parking lot, jumped in his Porsche, placed the Cup in the backseat, and drove off as a handful of fans roared outside.

Two generations have passed since a Red Wing hoisted the Cup, kissed it, paraded it around the ice and handed it off to his teammates and coaches. Yzerman's departure brought to a close one of the wildest nights in Detroit's history, one of the biggest parties in 42 years — since the last time the Wings had won the Cup. It capped a perfect evening.

"I don't know how to describe the way I feel," Yzerman said, enraptured in Stanley Cup bliss. "I'm glad the game is over, but I wish it never ended.

"Sometimes you hold your dream way out there and wonder if you can ever be as good as your dream. It was almost like I wanted to sit back and watch it all and not miss a minute of it."

There was so much to savor. The memories will last a lifetime. The final score of Game 4 of the 1997 Stanley Cup finals, 2-1, over Philadelphia, might well be forgotten. The goal scorers, Nicklas Lidstrom and Darren McCarty, could get lost in the telling of this tale to future generations.

BANNER SEASON (LEFT): The banner commemorating the Wings' championship season is raised as, from left, Brendan Shanahan, Nicklas Lidstrom and Steve Yzerman cheer. It was Detroit's first Stanley Cup season in 42 years.

GABRIEL B. TAIT

PARTY HEARTY: Darren McCarty and Martin Lapointe are up in arms after the Red Wings defeated Philadelphia in the Cup finals.

DREAM COME TRUE

"It was an honor to carry the Cup after Steve Yzerman."
Teammate Igor Larionov

MARY SCHROEDER

TRAVEL COMPANION: Being The Captain has its privileges. Yzerman took home the Stanley Cup after his team won the trophy in '97. He placed it into the backseat of his Porsche and drove off with fans applauding.

But the images of celebration on the ice and in the dressing room will never die. That's why grown men, battered and weary, hurl themselves in front of speeding pucks and shrug off sticks to the face. That's why they play the game.

At 11 p.m., Yzerman touched the Cup for the first time, raising it above his head and taking it to center ice where his teammates awaited.

Yzerman wasn't sure what to do. He asked coach Scotty Bowman — who was celebrating his seventh Cup as a coach, second-most in history — for advice, and Bowman sent Yzerman off on his counterclockwise trip around the rink. The coach made sure the rest of the team stayed behind.

This was the moment The Captain had waited for since he was drafted by the Wings fourth overall in 1983.

It was worth the wait. Yzerman skated back to the bench and gave the Cup to team owner Mike Ilitch, who held it high. Then Yzerman returned to the group and passed the Cup to Slava Fetisov and Igor Larionov, the Russian elder statesmen who left their homeland for a chance to play in the NHL. They carried the trophy around the ice together, waving to fans.

"I was surprised," Larionov said. "I play with Slava for many, many years and we wait for this for long time. It was an honor to carry the Cup after Steve Yzerman."

Yzerman finally admitted in an emotional moment that the whispers all these years have stung him, even if he never showed it.

"They always say, 'He's a good player, but he didn't win it,' " Yzerman said. "And now they can't say that anymore. No matter what, they can't say it, you know?...

"These past five years, there were summers where I didn't even want to go outside, I didn't want to be recognized, I put on my hat, my sunglasses, I walked around in a shell. You're embarrassed. I've felt that way before."

He flicked a champagne drop off his nose.

No more embarrassment. ☉

FREE SKATE: Yzerman touched the Stanley Cup for the first time at 11 p.m. on June 7. He didn't know what to do with it, until coach Scotty Bowman directed him to skate counterclockwise around the rink.

YZERMANIA

■ **What Yzerman said the night the Wings won the Stanley Cup:** "I was glad when the game was over, but then I didn't want the game to end. I've been watching hockey since I was 5 years old. I always dreamed of the day I would get the Stanley Cup. Sometimes I wondered if I would ever get there. As the game went on, it was almost as if I wanted to sit back and watch it."

BY OWEN DAVIS

■ **On winning the Cup:** "It was the one thing in my career I didn't have. I wanted dearly to have my name on the Stanley Cup before I retired."

■ **Skating with the Cup after the game:** "I would have preferred to go with everybody in the beginning. I wanted to go as one big group. As I went about halfway around, I thought, 'This thing is getting heavy.' My arm about fell off. I was looking for my parents and my wife and a friend in the corner. I wanted to make sure I saw them as I was carrying it around the rink. I just tried to take it all in....

"It was the greatest moment in my career, the most gratifying and the most rewarding."

■ **Passing the Cup to Slava Fetisov, who held it with Igor Larionov:** "The last couple of days I thought who I wanted to give the Cup to. I thought about Slava. He and Igor, what they stand for, are good examples for younger players. He has been through a lot in his career. If he's not coming back, this is the ultimate....

"All five Russian players were significant players and great guys."

■ **Seeing Scotty Bowman in skates on the ice:** "That was great. I've seen it all. He doesn't show emotion. He doesn't let us get too close to him. For a few minutes there, he was one of us."

■ **The fans:** "I know for the city it's pride. You can walk around, and Detroit is the Stanley Cup champion. The fans are the Stanley Cup champions. You can hold your head up high. We broke some hearts, but they kept coming back." ●

TV TIME: Yzerman and the Cup were guests on the "Late Show with David Letterman" in 1998.

SHINING MOMENT

CRAIG PORTER

RIDING HIGH: Everyone loves a parade, including Slava Fetisov, a key player on the Red Wings' championship team.

Pay no attention to the calendar. By proclamation of the captain of the Stanley Cup champion Detroit Red Wings — has a nice ring to it, eh? — summer began Tuesday, June 10, 1997.

With a magnificent parade.

It began, as it should have, with the cantankerous coach, who surely knows the recipe for a winner, riding next to his wife, Suella, in the back of a white convertible.

Scotty Bowman was beaming proudly.

It ended, also as it should have, with Steve Yzerman standing triumphantly in the last of 25 matching red convertibles, the Stanley Cup held high over his head.

The night before, at a gathering at Joe Louis Arena that gave thousands of season-ticket holders, suite holders and sponsors first dibs on all the new championship souvenirs, Yzerman ended a stirring speech by saying: "Let's all enjoy the most wonderful summer of our lives."◗

SHATTERED

"I'm concerned. I've got to make sure my boys are taken care of."

Mike Ilitch, after two Wings players and the team masseur were seriously injured in an accident

TRAGEDY AFTER TRIUMPH: A limousine crash ended the career of Red Wings defenseman Vladimir Konstantinov six days after Detroit won the 1997 Stanley Cup. He was in a coma for more than a month after suffering head injuries.

WILLIAM ARCHIE

Less than a week after winning the Stanley Cup, two of the Red Wings' Russian stars and the team's Russian masseur were seriously injured when a limousine in which they were riding ran off Woodward Avenue and crashed into a tree in Birmingham.

Vladimir Konstantinov, 30, was in a coma in critical condition with head injuries and breathing with the aid of a ventilator at William Beaumont Hospital in Royal Oak.

The masseur, Sergei Mnatsakanov, 43, was in critical condition, undergoing surgery for a compressed skull. Defenseman Slava Fetisov, 39, was in fair condition with a chest injury and a bruised lung but was able to talk. The limousine driver was in fair condition.

The one-car accident was reported to Birmingham police at 9:13 p.m. June 13 on Woodward about 400 yards south of Big Beaver. Both front air bags of the white stretch limo deployed when the car careered off southbound Woodward into the grassy median of the divided road and hit the tree, crumpling the front end. The impact uprooted the tree.

The crash came on the heels of a jubilant week for the team, which clinched its first NHL championship in 42 years.

MARY SCHROEDER

NOT ALONE: The Red Wings rallied around their Russian teammate, defenseman Vladimir Konstantinov, after the limousine he was traveling in crashed.

Red Wings owner Mike Ilitch arrived at the hospital at about 10:45 p.m., dressed in a team windbreaker. He said he heard about the accident on television.

"I'm concerned," he said. "I've got to make sure my boys are taken care of."

John Wharton, the Red Wings' trainer, arrived and ran into the hospital around 11:30, followed by captain Steve Yzerman and Brendan Shanahan. Other players followed.

Mathieu Dandenault, a forward, said the team was at a golf outing at the Orchards at 28 Mile and Van Dyke.

The two players and the masseur decided to leave about an hour and a half before the rest of the team, which was to regroup at Chris Osgood's home in Birmingham, he said.

When the rest of the players got in the limos, Yzerman's cell phone rang with news of the accident, Dandenault said. Yzerman gathered the team and let them all know what had happened.

"From what Stevie said, he's fighting for his life," Dandenault said of Konstantinov. "It was the worst feeling ever."Ⓖ

THOUGHTS OF HOME

BY MITCH ALBOM

And still, the sun shone brightly. How could this be? Shouldn't there have been clouds and rain? How could hockey fans reconcile perfect weather on Father's Day with the image of Vladimir Konstantinov÷ lying motionless in a hospital bed, breathing through a respirator, a brain monitor in his head?

Real life doesn't play favorites.

So while the sun shone Sunday afternoon, Red Wings players who would have otherwise been out golfing, partying, taking the Stanley Cup home to friends and family, instead were in a sterile room, visiting their fallen teammate, playing him music — "We are the Champions" — hoping something would shake him from his injured sleep.

Meanwhile, Detroit sports fans spent the day in conflicting emotions, laughing at barbecues and playing with their children, then suddenly getting serious, dropping their voices and saying, "Any news on Vladdie? Is he going to be all right?"

The truth is no one knows whether he's going to be all right. That limo accident that threw Konstantinov into a coma was serious business — not serious sports business but serious life-and-death business. It is especially hard to imagine the popular Konstantinov — who took and gave so much physical punishment in his job — laid low by such an accident.

Recently, I finally got him to sit down and do a radio interview on WJR. He had been hesitant because of his English, but he was funny and relaxed, and winning the championship seemed to boost his confidence. He marveled at the fans who had come to cheer at the Wings' parade. And when I asked whether he planned to take the Cup home for his two days with it over the summer, he winked and said, "Yes, home to West Bloomfield."

"Not Russia?" I joked.

"Too far," he said, laughing. "By time I get there, I have to come back."

That was six days ago. And today we're not talking about Russia, or even West Bloomfield.

Today we would be happy if he were able to just sit up and smile.

BELIEVE!

"Everything we did all year, we did for this guy. We never stopped believing."

Igor Larionov, after the Red Wings repeated as Stanley Cup champions

BY MITCH ALBOM

1998

JUNE 16

WASHINGTON — The first one they won for the city. This one they won for their hearts. A hockey saga that began last summer in yelps of joy, and was interrupted six days later by tears of sadness, has worked itself back around to joy once more, with Red Wings players in a happy mob around the net, another Stanley Cup in tow. But this one was different. It was hard-fought, it was tiring, it was long and sometimes painful. But it was always meant to be. We can see that now. What happened here was less about victory than it was about belief.

And so, when the hockey ended, even as the pundits were banging out notes about a Detroit dynasty, even as fans back home were screaming themselves hoarse, the Wings were doing what they had dreamed of doing all year long.

Finally, with tears in their eyes, they handed the Stanley Cup to their fallen colleague, Vladimir Konstantinov, and that tells you all you need to know about this team. They weren't playing for themselves. They were playing for a higher cause — and it took them to the highest heights.

"TWO! TWO! TWO!" yelled the Wings, as they posed for their first

NICO TOUTENHOOFD

SHANNYTOWN: Brendan Shanahan is the center of attention as the Red Wings celebrate their Stanley Cup victory.

FOR VLADDIE: Slava Fetisov, left, Steve Yzerman, center, and Igor Larionov rally around Vladimir Konstantinov after winning the 1998 Stanley Cup. Konstantinov was injured in a limousine crash six days after he won the Stanley Cup with the 1997 squad.

GABRIEL B. TAIT

VICTORY CIGAR: Vladimir Konstantinov and Slava Fetisov share a moment after the Red Wings win the Stanley Cup on June 16, 1998.

> "A year ago ... doctors were telling us maybe Vladdie will live, maybe he'll die."
>
> Yzerman

photo as 1998 champions gathered around Konstantinov in his wheelchair, the Cup in his lap, a victory cigar in his fingers, an unbelievable smile on his face.

"Everything we did all year, we did for this guy," Igor Larionov said. "We never stopped believing."

Believe and you can fly. Isn't that the theme of songs and stories about bravery and heroes? So here was Konstantinov, crippled in a limousine crash with team masseur Sergei Mnatsakanov six days after last year's Cup, making the trip to Washington, perhaps because he knew, in his heart, that this would be the moment. He sat all game long in Section 116 in the MCI Center, over a homemade sign that read, "Do You Believe?"

Konstantinov watched the first period, as Sergei Fedorov, his Russian friend, spun and drew defenders, then dished to Doug Brown, who whacked a puck past Washington's Olaf Kolzig. 1-0.

He watched the second period as Larionov, his Russian friend, dished to Martin Lapointe, who whacked a puck past Kolzig. 2-0.

He watched as Larry Murphy fired another puck past Kolzig. And as Brown put in his second of the

night.

He watched as Chris Osgood turned back nearly every devil's stone the Capitals fired in his direction.

He watched as his former teammates dug all game long, in the corners, against the boards, in the deepest part of their hearts, to end this odyssey the way they wanted.

And finally, when the horn sounded and the scoreboard read Detroit 4, Washington 1, he watched as, one by one, they skated over to him, hugged him, told him to use this to get better, maybe the most noble use this Cup will ever see.

Believe? How could you not?

"You know today is June 16," said Steve Yzerman, who was a unanimous choice for the Conn Smythe Trophy as best player in the playoffs, "and I remember a year ago we were sitting in a room at Beaumont Hospital and doctors were telling us maybe Vladdie will live, maybe he'll die. And here were are one year later and he's at the arena with us, getting the Stanley Cup. I think it's been... it's the most emotional moment I'll ever be involved in." ●

TWO MUCH: After a 42-year drought, Yzerman and the Red Wings take hold of the Cup for the second time in two years.

MVP

WASHINGTON — Steve Yzerman, who hoisted the Stanley Cup with a sense of relief in 1997, lifted Lord Stanley's chalice a second time and, in the process, removed the final burden from his shoulders. He proved then that he can lead. This time, he proved he can star as well.

BY DREW SHARP

Any questions that might have remained regarding his talent or toughness were answered decisively when he carried off the Conn Smythe Trophy as the playoffs' most valuable player. As if there was any contest.

Yzerman's consistency carried the Wings through Sergei Fedorov's and Brendan Shanahan's offensive peaks and valleys. The Cup-clinching 4-1 victory over Washington marked the first time in the past two Stanley Cup finals that Yzerman didn't register a point in a game. By the look on his face afterward, it didn't bother him.

"Yeah, there's a certain amount of gratification in having my name included on a trophy with so many great players," said Yzerman, who had six goals among a team-leading 24 points in the playoffs. "When I first came into the league, I don't think there were many people who could correctly spell or pronounce my name. Winning this award along with the Stanley Cup definitely is a nice stamp on my career."

New York Rangers general manager Neil Smith scouted Yzerman for the Wings in the 1983 draft. Few others have his special insight into Yzerman's evolution as a total team player.

"It's amazing he's still one of the best players in the whole playoffs at 33 years of age," Smith said. "He's been amazing. I think he's better now than he was earlier in his career. He's a way-more-complete player, a better player."

"Stevie's never really gotten the big recognition that the Gretzkys and Lemieuxs always got," teammate Martin Lapointe said. "We've always known what a great player and great leader he is, but winning two straight Stanley Cups would have to convince others of that, as well."

"Most fans didn't know this was the first really big trophy you've ever won," someone said to a champagne-soaked Yzerman. "Is it better when the awards come later in your career?"

"Well, I think I'd appreciate it anytime," he answered.

"But it really means a lot to have the Yzerman name on the Conn Smythe. I mean, just for my dad to know the Yzerman name is there." ©

MARQUEE PLAYER: Yzerman carts the Conn Smythe Trophy down Woodward Avenue during the Red Wings' victory parade.

KIRTHMON F. DOZIER

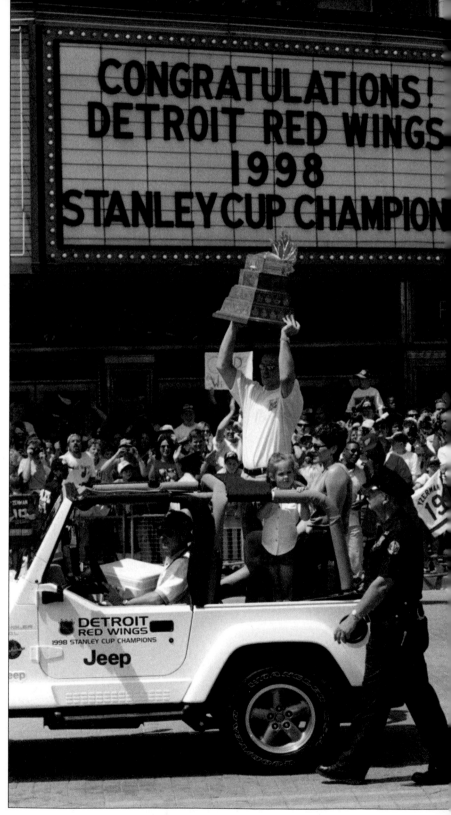

JULIAN H. GONZALEZ

OLD PALS: Another Stanley Cup win meant another trip to the White House for Steve Yzerman and the Wings to meet with President Bill Clinton. When the president suggested that Yzerman should run for office, he replied, "I would, but I don't like the pay."

FOLLOW THE LEADER

BY HELENE
ST. JAMES

1999
JANUARY 28

They joked with each other like two old friends — the leader of the free world and the captain of the Red Wings. Each had a lot to say. Each clearly admires the other.

The exchanges between President Bill Clinton and Steve Yzerman highlighted a decidedly familiar affair at the White House. The 30-minute ceremony began with a down-home greeting by Clinton, who started by saying, "Welcome back to the White House."

Jokes pervaded the Wings' second visit to the White House as Stanley Cup champions. Clinton told a packed East Room that their presence there was becoming such a routine that he would invite them every time he hosted a Michigan Day.

Yzerman displayed his wit a few moments later after presenting Clinton with a Wings road jersey bearing Clinton's name and No. 98.

"Now when you and Hillary settle down to watch hockey on television, you can both wear a jersey," Yzerman said. Last year he gave Clinton a white home jersey — which Clinton said he used.

"I wore it around the house until Hillary pointed out I wasn't as broad-shouldered as she thought I was," Clinton said with a laugh.

But the best exchange between Clinton and Yzerman came after the cameras were turned off. As he was leaving, Clinton stopped by Yzerman and, according to witnesses, told him he is a good speaker and should run for office.

Yzerman quipped, "I would, but I don't like the pay."

Yzerman is thrilled to have pictures of himself with the president. He remembered when he got last year's photos.

"I got a note sent to my home with his signature on it and on White House stationery," Yzerman said. "That's something I want to frame and put up on my wall.

"Actually meeting and shaking hands with the president was a bigger deal than I thought it would be. It was pretty impressive just to be around him, just standing in a room and watching the president of the U.S. was much bigger than I thought it would be. So, yeah, I really enjoyed it."

Yzerman summed up the experience perfectly.

"It would be a nice habit if we could keep coming back, but they might get sick of us here," he said. "Hopefully we get another opportunity to get back here."

> "Actually meeting and shaking hands with the president was a bigger deal than I thought it would be."
> The Captain after meeting The President

CAN'T WIN 'EM ALL

"I really felt like something slipped away."
Yzerman, after the Wings failed to bring home a third straight Cup

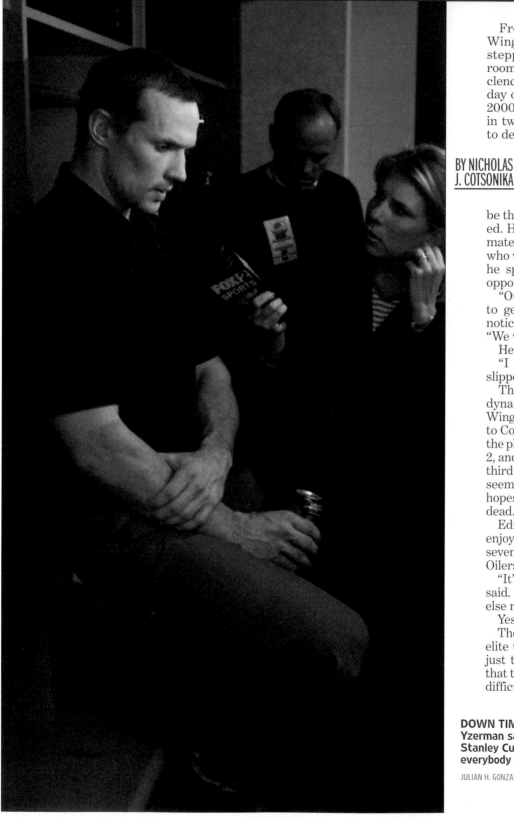

BY NICHOLAS J. COTSONIKA

Fresh from the shower, Red Wings captain Steve Yzerman stepped outside the dressing room, tugged on his Tigers cap and clenched his teeth. It was the first day of training camp for the 1999-2000 season, and for the first time in two years, he wasn't preparing to defend the Stanley Cup.

The feeling must have been strange, a bit painful, knowing that Dallas was on top, knowing that the Wings would be the hunters instead of the hunted. He looked around at his teammates, mostly the same old guys who won Cups in 1997 and '98, and he spoke of last season's missed opportunities.

"Our whole year was a struggle to get going," said Yzerman, not noticing as fans screamed for him. "We were tired."

He looked down. He frowned.

"I really felt like something slipped away."

There is no more talk of a dynasty in Detroit because the Wings lost four consecutive games to Colorado in the second round of the playoffs, dropping the series, 4-2, and didn't come home with their third straight Cup. But pessimism seems awfully odd. The Wings' hopes for greatness are far from dead.

Edmonton, the last NHL team to enjoy a dynasty, won five Cups in seven years from '84 to '90. But the Oilers never won three straight.

"It's kind of humbling," Yzerman said. "We're just like everybody else now."

Yes and no.

The Wings are still very much an elite team, the class of more than just the Central Division. It's just that their third Cup would be more difficult to win than their first. ⊝

DOWN TIME: "It is kind of humbling," Yzerman said about not winning the Stanley Cup in 1999. "We are just like everybody else now."

JULIAN H. GONZALEZ

GOLDEN BOY

DAVID P. GILKEY

CANADIAN GLORY: Yzerman, left, and Brendan Shanahan, right, earned the gold with the Canadian hockey team during the 2002 Winter Games in Salt Lake City. They defeated Red Wings teammates Chris Chelios, second from left, and Brett Hull of Team USA, 5-2.

BY NICHOLAS J. COTSONIKA

2002
FEBRUARY 24

WEST VALLEY CITY, Utah — As the clock counted down on Canada's 5-2 victory over the United States, Canadian fans broke out in song. And not just any song. They sang "O Canada" loud and proud. "God keep our land glorious and free...."

"It gave us chills," said Canada's Brendan Shanahan, a Red Wings forward.

Then the buzzer sounded, and it was over, the game, the tournament, the torment. As coach Pat Quinn said, Canadians feel they invented hockey, developed hockey, taught hockey to the world. Now they had the Olympic men's hockey gold medal. For the first time in half a century.

"It's a huge victory," said Canada's Steve Yzerman, the Wings' captain. "Hockey, it's the No. 1 sport in Canada, the most popular sport. So we're thrilled to be Olympic champions."

While the Canadians celebrated, the Americans watched. But after a few minutes, captain Chris Chelios, a Wings defenseman, led the team to center ice. The players raised their sticks to the crowd in unison, and the American fans cheered.

Joe Sakic gave the Canadians a 3-2 lead on a second-period power play, and the goal would prove to be the game-winner. At 18:40 of the third period, when Sakic scored Canada's fifth goal, Yzerman jumped to his feet on the bench and hugged a couple of teammates. The fans started singing the anthem. "True patriot love...."

The teams lined up and shook hands. Shanahan and Yzerman hugged Chelios and Brett Hull. The Americans congratulated the Canadians; the Canadians consoled the Americans.

"You know, it doesn't prove that Canada's the best," Yzerman said. "We're just Olympic champions, that's all."

Yzerman grabbed teammate Owen Nolan's video camera and taped Nolan receiving his medal, then he gave it back and received his medal with a big smile. Early in his career, Yzerman was cut from Canada Cup teams. He thought Nagano in 1998 might have been his last shot at Olympic glory. Now he was a national hero more than ever before.

"It's a great moment," he said. ◗

> "It's a huge victory.... We're thrilled to be Olympic champions."
> Gold medal winner Steve Yzerman

THE 'C' IS FOR CHARACTER

"You can't take advantage of your status. ... It creates dissension."
The Captain

BY MITCH ALBOM

2002
MAY 10

Steve Yzerman is in his car, driving to practice between games 4 and 5 of the Western Conference semifinals. He doesn't really do much on the practice ice these days. For one thing, his bad knee can't take it. And, anyhow, at this point in the season, he and the other veterans don't exactly need work.

But he goes.

He goes because "you're supposed to be there," he says. "If we have an 11 a.m. practice, it's not like I can show up at 11:15 and say, 'Hey, Scotty, how you doin'?' You can't take advantage of your status. Other guys won't say anything because they don't want to rock the boat, but they start wondering why they should be doing it if you're not. It creates dissension."

Funny. Another star athlete, the NBA's Allen Iverson — 10 years younger than Yzerman — complained that his coach, Larry Brown, was making too much of his skipping practices.

"I'm the franchise player and we're talking about practice?" an angry Iverson said. "Practice?... We're talking about practice?"

Well, actually, they were talking about character.

Which is what Iverson has to learn and Yzerman doesn't. It almost oozes from him now. So much so that some observers tend to look at The Captain these days and all but gush, like the TV announcers who keep insisting that he is playing "on one leg."

Not quite. If you play on one leg, you fall down. Yzerman is not a crippled, crawling-out-of-bed martyr.

"I have a sore knee, and that's about it," he says. "It hasn't gotten better, but it hasn't gotten worse. I'm not playing on one leg or anything. That's just... ah... you know."

We know. It's a compliment.
You like to give Yzerman com-

MANDI WRIGHT

pliments, partly because he hates getting them so much. In Game 4 of the semifinals, against St. Louis, he played the kind of game that pushes teams to glory. Yes, he scored a goal, but the points mattered least.

It was the effort. It was the resilience. It was the storm of collisions he weathered, many by design of the Blues, who wanted to nullify him. Couldn't do it. They tried. Nobody harder than mammoth defenseman Chris Pronger, who attempted a slam that Yzerman evaded by ducking low like someone out of a Jackie Chan movie. Pronger flipped over him and landed on his right knee and out of the playoffs with a torn ACL.

"That was a fluky thing," Yzerman says from his car. "You don't want to see anyone get hurt."

So it was a good night for Yzerman — and, to boot, it was his 37th birthday. He flew back with the team, got in his car and drove home. If he were proud of himself, it could be expected. After all, playing among kids 10 and 15 years younger, he was perhaps the best player out there.

So how did he celebrate?

"Actually," he says, approaching downtown Detroit, "the only thought I gave to my birthday was that when I came into the league, the Wings had just acquired Brad Park. And I had always looked up to Brad Park. But he was 37 at the time. I thought, 'Wow. He's 37. He's got a wife and family. He's an old guy.' And now that's me."

He laughs and through the cell phone you hear the wind from outside. You realize this is slowly coming to an end, this era of veterans like Yzerman, sticking in one city their whole careers, going to practice on sunny days without complaint.

He is, so far, having the playoffs of his dreams, leading the Red Wings in goals, points, game-winners — and respect. ◗

HANG 10

LEAVING ON A HIGH NOTE: Coach Scotty Bowman and captain Steve Yzerman welcome the Stanley Cup back to Detroit in 2002 after beating the Carolina Hurricanes. After the win, Bowman whispered, "Mike, it's time for me to go."

BY MITCH ALBOM

2002

JUNE 13

The gloves were tossed, the confetti came down, and into the happy heap they flew, the old guys and the new guys and the 41-year-olds and the 21-year-olds and the guys who just got a second or third championship and the guys who finally got their first. They leaped over the top. They barreled in from the side.

Yzerman on top of Datsyuk on top of Lidstrom on top of Hasek. Fedorov on top of Hull on top of Devereaux on top of Larionov. Old on new. Veteran on rookie. And in that delirious, if somewhat toothless stack of players, the Detroit Red Wings evoked their team philosophy: In a pileup, everybody is a star.

And that's just the way they like it.

They came. They clicked. They conquered. The Greatest Hockey Roster Ever Assembled just finished the kind of season that leaves

JULIAN H. GONZALEZ

WELCOME BACK: Yzerman and Sergei Fedorov celebrate Brendan Shanahan's second-period goal during Game 5 of the Stanley Cup finals against the Carolina Hurricanes at Joe Louis Arena. It was the trio's third Cup season with the Wings.

fans weeping with satisfaction. These Detroit players carried a dream from the opening night in October to the closing horn in June, when the final foe, the Carolina Hurricanes, was vanquished. And in all that time, not once did their dream exceed three colors: red, white — and silver.

Welcome back, Stanley.

"Everybody on this team at some point stepped up for a big play in a big game," said joyous captain Steve Yzerman, after lifting the Stanley Cup, the most precious trophy in all of sports, for the third time in his career. "The only thing that mattered was winning, and the only thing that mattered was the team."

And this, folks, was a team for the ages — and one that will never be the same because, moments after the final horn, Scotty Bowman, who brought Detroit three championships in six years, whispered in his owner's ear, "Mike, it's time for me to go."

He leaves on the highest of notes, having steered a veteran-heavy group that never faltered, never panicked and never seemed to tire. The Red Wings overcame the hottest team in hockey in the first round, a supposedly blistering goalie in the second, the defending NHL champions in the third, and the most dangerous kind of upstarts in the finals. Not one opponent resembled the other — except in the way they all ended, skating off, shaking their heads,

EVERYONE'S A WINNER: The Red Wings gather around captain Steve Yzerman, who led the team to the 2002 Stanley Cup.

JULIAN H. GONZALEZ

"Everybody on this team at some point stepped up for a big play in a big game." Yzerman

marveling at the tank that had just rolled over them.

They came. The new additions. Dominik Hasek from Buffalo, Luc Robitaille from Los Angeles, Brett Hull from Dallas, Fredrik Olausson from Sweden, Pavel Datsyuk from Russia. All arrived with a single goal in mind: to reach the top of the heap by the end of the season.

They clicked. New players mixing with old. Young players learning from veterans. Czechs, Swedes, Canadians, Russians and Americans, leaving their egos at the door, dropping their superstar name tags, heeding the instructions of coaching legend Scotty Bowman and morphing under the quiet leadership of Steve Yzerman.

They conquered. Best record in hockey. Vancouver, St. Louis, Colorado and Carolina in the playoffs.

In the end, Shanahan pummeled into Yzerman in a football bang that knocked them both to the ice, and the noise inside the Joe threatened to shake the rust off the rafters.

"I saw Steve later and his nose was bleeding," Shanahan said in the Wings' champagne-soaked locker room. "And I said, 'What happened? Did you get high-sticked?'

"And Steve said, 'No, I think you broke my nose when you hugged me.' "

Well, can you blame him?

Lord Stanley was back in Detroit for the third time in six years, and the 10th time in history. We're a double-digit town now.◉

THE PERFECT MIX: Veteran Wings and new Wings clicked in 2002, scoring the best record in hockey and a Stanley Cup championship.

JULIAN H. GONZALEZ

FINAL SHIFT

THE CAPTAIN'S LAST RUN

Yzerman has been slogging the same commute to work since Ronald Reagan's first term as president, driving in, heading toward the river, pulling in the corner lot.

JULIAN H. GONZALEZ

THE AFTERMATH: Yzerman, wearing a visor to protect his left eye, played his first game of the 2005-06 season on Oct. 26 at Joe Louis against Chicago. Yzerman's eye was badly injured after he was hit by a puck in May 2004 (facing page).

He gets the best parking spot. That's one perk. Over the years, he jokes, his space has moved "closer and closer" to the Joe Louis Arena door and now "I only get bumped for two people."

BY MITCH ALBOM

"Mr. Ilitch being one?" I say.

"And his wife being the other," he laughs.

Forget 23 years with the same team. How about 23 years in the same building? Steve Yzerman has been slogging the same commute to work since Ronald Reagan's first term as president, driving in, heading toward the river, pulling in the corner lot. In that way, he is truly like the factory workers who so admire him. And after all these years, he is entitled to retire with benefits.

We sit down to talk. There is much to talk about. There is much to put into perspective.

But wait. Here comes Gordie Howe. Carrying a small dog, he walks through the lounge where we are conversing. And suddenly, the two most famous figures in the history of Red Wings hockey are inches apart.

"Hi, Gordie."

"Congratulations, Steve."

"Thank you."

"You got that old quickness back, huh?"

Yzerman laughs. "Some days. Some days."

Howe moves closer.

"The cake is made," he says, "now you gotta put on the icing."

Thanks. I can go home now.

How much better perspective can

you get than that? The cake is made? Now put on the icing? Doesn't that apply not only to the 2005-06 season but to The Captain's illustrious career as well? The cake has been his 23 years, three championships, 692 goals and immeasurable endurance. The icing would have been a fourth Stanley Cup over his head.

At nearly 41 entering the 2006 playoffs, he was a monument to resiliency, but even he was a few breaths away from hanging it up. In November and December of 2005, he admitted, "There were times when I was like, 'What did I do here?'... Games were going by. I felt terrible out there. ... I'd get the puck and look up and I felt like I was playing against 10 guys."

But, true to form, he willed things

to change. Despite enough nagging injuries to slow an army, despite a knee that should have gotten out of the sports business a long time ago, Yzerman rallied to play better and better in 2005-06, urging himself to a level of excellence that is, if not his dream standard, at least acceptable.

And more than acceptable to anyone else.

Yzerman had 14 points in the last 13 games of the 2005-06 regular season. That's giant-sized for a guy half his age. He would hunker down to his favorite time of year, when, as he puts it, "it's all sleeping, eating and playing." And while he calls himself "not really" nostalgic ("just about my children"), there was a heightened sense of appreciation this time — for what would be his last playoff run.

Perhaps it was the 2004-05 lockout. Or maybe it was the ignoble ending in the 2004 postseason against Calgary, when a puck hit his face, broke his orbital bone, almost blinded him and finished him for the playoffs.

"I really enjoy the atmosphere now, the tension, the emotional highs and lows" of the playoffs, he says. "That's the thing that, iron-

MOMENT OF IMPACT: Yzerman is consumed by pain after being hit in the face with a puck on May 1, 2004. The Wings were playing Calgary in Game 5 of the Western Conference semifinals. Yzerman underwent 4½ hours of surgery to repair his left eye.

DAVID P. GILKEY

SOME OF THE CAPTAIN'S INJURIES

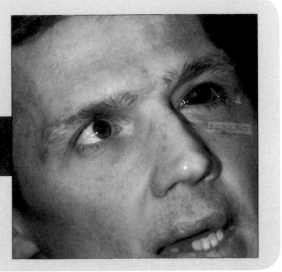

▌ **1985-86:** Broken collarbone. Missed last 29 games.

▌ **1987-88:** Knee injury. Missed final 16 games, 13 in playoffs.

▌ **1993-94:** Herniated disk. Missed 26 games.

▌ **1998-99:** Suffered fractured nose and severe cuts after taking a point-blank shot to the face from Paul Coffey. Missed All-Star Game.

▌ **2000-01:** Arthroscopic knee surgery and foot injury. Missed 22 games and most of playoffs.

▌ **2002-03:** Underwent osteotomy, a knee realignment surgery that had never been done on a professional athlete. Missed first 66 games.

▌ **2003-04:** Suffered orbital bone fracture after getting hit in the eye with a puck in the playoffs against Calgary.

▌ **2005-06:** Groin injury slowed him early in the season. Missed Games 4 and 5 in the first round, but played in Game 6 vs. the Edmonton Oilers with a torn oblique muscle.

THE CAPTAIN'S LAST RUN

"When I came in, I thought John Ogrodnick was old – and I think he was 26!"
Yzerman, reflecting on the early days

ically, as you get older, you get more comfortable with. You get less scared of it."

You also stop taking it for granted.

It wasn't that way, of course, when a boyish, long-haired Yzerman was being scouted by the Red Wings in 1983 and he came to Detroit for just the second time in his life.

"Jimmy Devellano and Nick Polano, I think, took me around," Yzerman recalls. "We toured the arena. I was kind of overwhelmed with such a big city. We went to a Tigers game. We ate at Joe Muer's restaurant over on Gratiot."

He shakes his head at the memory. Tiger Stadium is empty. The restaurant is gone. But Yzerman is still here, in his old building. Back then, he thought, the Wings would win Stanley Cups for sure, right away, lots of them. Instead, he went through a long drought of mediocre teams, some so bad they earned the nickname Dead Wings.

"Do you remember, when you first arrived, how old you thought a 40-year-old person was?" I ask.

"When I came in," he says, smiling, "I thought John Ogrodnick was old — and I think he was 26!... Brad Park was 37,

and I looked up to him as a kind of father figure."

And now, with the younger Red Wings, I ask, do they see you that way?

"Oh, it's like I'm ancient, yeah. They don't want to go for dinner where I go to dinner. They don't want to see the movies I want to see. ... Music. They're all into hip-hop and I just don't get it."

What music are you into?

He laughs. "The same music you're into."

And that's the thing about Yzerman, isn't it? The young fans admire him because he's The Captain. The older fans admire him because he handles it

TIME FLIES: Yzerman turned 33 in 1998, the same year he played in this playoff game against St. Louis.

with dignity. And people his own age admire him because he listens to their music — yet he's still out there, banging with the kids. I mean, how do you not like a guy who moans of his young teammates: "They don't even know who Led Zeppelin is."

Still, if there is one nuance to the big picture of Steve Yzerman, it is not his age, his statistics or even his celebrated leadership. It's his adaptability. Many great players come down the pike, but they are often great only as long as they keep doing what they do.

Yzerman was drafted, in the early 1980s, as a playmaking center. He became a goal-scorer when the team needed offense, and he racked up big points for the next 10 years. In the middle '90s he shifted under Scotty Bowman to a more defensive

GO WITH THE FLOW: Stevie Y, celebrating a goal against Toronto in 1993, was a master of adaptation. Throughout his career, he changed to help his team, adapting a more defensive style of play in the mid-'90s.

MARY SCHROEDER

Isiah Thomas

Barry Sanders

Alan Trammell

Gordie Howe

YZERMAN: OUR FAVORITE

In 2004, Steve Yzerman was ruled king of Michigan sports.

Fifteen percent of Michiganders named Yzerman as Detroit's favorite sports hero in the last 20 years, according to a 2004 survey of 600 registered voters by EPIC/MRA of Lansing.

Next closest was Barry Sanders with 10%, Al Kaline with 9% and Isiah Thomas with 8%. The only other hockey player to get more than 1% was Gordie Howe with 5%.

In a separate question asking respondents to choose from a list of six recent stars, Yzerman was the big favorite with 31%. Thomas was second with 14%, followed by Sanders (13%), Alan Trammell (12%), Joe Dumars (8%) and Bill Laimbeer (4%).

JULIAN H. GONZALEZ

WORK HAZARDS: Yzerman is thrown off balance after taking a hit during the 2005-06 season, his final year in the NHL.

KIRTHMON F. DOZIER

THE CAPTAIN'S LAST RUN

style. And as his knee injuries limited his cuts and turns, he became a stronger, grinding, offensive presence, more likely to poke in a goal than to speed-deliver one.

"I try to keep in straight lines now, let the puck do the work," he says. "And there's very little one-on-one stuff anymore. ... It's really just because of my knee, not age. Every now and then I'll feel good and try to do something and it just ain't happening. And I'll realize, 'Calm down a little bit.' "

It is rare a player can handle that, much less thrive despite it.

Yzerman did.

You think of how many years he has not been the team leader in points, or goals, or assists or pure skill — and yet he has never not been the team leader. ⊙

LIKE YZERMAN, LINDSAY CAME BACK FOR MORE

Steve Yzerman returned to the Red Wings in October 2005 after a full season lost to the lockout.

Ted Lindsay knows a little about how he feels.

BY BILL DOW

More than 40 years earlier, four years after retiring as the third-leading scorer in NHL history, Lindsay played for the Red Wings at the age of 39.

The circumstances were far different, though.

Yzerman was 40 and had access to year-round, state-of-the-art training facilities and strength coaches.

In Lindsay's day, NHL players held a second job in the off-season to make ends meet, and elliptical cross-training regimens were decades away from common use.

Lindsay's comeback in 1964 was one of the most remarkable in sports. Most players back then retired in their early 30s. But Lindsay did something other former players didn't. He stayed in shape.

A record opening-night crowd of 14,323 jammed Olympia Stadium, five weeks after the Beatles played there. Lindsay, wearing No. 15 instead of his famous No. 7 sweater, skated out to a standing ovation that lasted several minutes.

Although the Wings lost to the Maple Leafs, 5-3, and Lindsay didn't score, the left winger quickly demonstrated that the nickname Terrible Ted still applied. Lindsay, one of the toughest players of all time, received a 10-minute misconduct penalty in the second period for fighting with Tim Horton. ⊙

TERRIBLE TED: Lindsay was a card in 1964, the year he unretired.

CAPTAIN COMEBACK

"I really enjoyed being back on the ice. It's not perfect, but generally I was pleased." Yzerman, who hadn't played since June 13, 2002, the night he won his third Cup

BY NICHOLAS J. COTSONIKA

2003
FEBRUARY 24

He stepped onto the ice at 7, the 12th Red Wing through the door for warm-ups, and the fans who had come early cheered. He skated some laps. He shot some pucks. The music blared.

Then came the official word: He was playing. He was back. Steve Yzerman, the captain, the mayor of Hockeytown, whose image graced the Cadillac Tower in the heart of the city, was making an unprecedented return from knee realignment surgery.

When he emerged from the Joe Louis Arena tunnel for the game at 7:35, the rink was nearly full, and the fans rose to their feet. They stayed silent for the most part as he stood by the bench for the national anthem, but then they roared.

And when he hopped off the bench for the first time 54 seconds into the first period, centering Boyd Devereaux and Luc Robitaille, just wanting linesman Ray Scapinello to drop the puck quickly so he could take his first face-off and get going, the fans rose to their feet again and roared some more.

"STE-VIE!" they chanted. "STE-VIE!"

"I really enjoyed being back out on the ice," Yzerman said after the Wings' 5-4 victory over the Los Angeles Kings. "It's not perfect, but generally I was pleased with how I felt. I felt actually better than I expected."

Yzerman improved as the game progressed. He played 13:17 — 3:46 in the first period, 5:22 in the second and 4:09 in the third.

He skated with different linemates, sometimes at center, sometimes at right wing. He took no shots and had no points, but he was plus-1 and won nine of 15 face-offs — the last in the Detroit zone with 23.8 seconds left.

BACK IN ACTION: Detroit cheered when Yzerman returned to the ice on February 24, 2003, after knee surgery had benched him.
KIRTHMON F. DOZIER

When he fell, he got up. When a scrum formed, he got involved. And when it was over, he said he expected no problem in the morning.

Yzerman hadn't played since June 13, 2002. The Wings won the Stanley Cup that night, and in the commotion, with confetti still falling, he said, "What do you think would happen if I announced my retirement right now?"

Many men in Yzerman's shoes would have walked away.

It would have been a fitting finale to a Hall of Fame career: In a matter of months, he had won an Olympic gold medal for Canada and his third Stanley Cup for the Wings, and he had done it at age 37 — despite unspeakable hardship.

His right knee was wrecked. He tore his posterior cruciate ligament in 1988 and didn't have it reconstructed. He wore away his cartilage over the years until bone ground against bone. Two games into the playoffs, the Wings weren't sure he could go on — but he went on, leading them on and off the ice, although he needed constant treatment, took countless injections, had trouble scaling the steps to the team plane and hardly left his home or hotel rooms.

Walking hurt. Even standing hurt. The knee ached all the time.

"He's a freak of nature," said John Wharton, then the Wings' trainer, who learned to worry mostly about Yzerman's swelling and range of motion. "I think he has a different nervous system than the rest of us. I don't think he processes pain." ⓖ

KIRTHMON F. DOZIER

SUPERMAN: Yzerman came back strong from off-season knee surgery. He helped the Wings beat the Los Angeles Kings, 5-4.

SCENES FROM YZERMAN'S RETURN

▌ **Welcome back:** Steve Yzerman got a standing ovation as fans realized he had rushed out of the gate and begun circling in Detroit's zone.

▌ **Last-minute check:** As Karen Newman prepared to sing "The Star-Spangled Banner," Yzerman handed his helmet to Red Wings equipment manager Paul Boyer for a quick fix. He got it back just as the anthem ended.

▌ **Paging No. 19:** Yzerman began his first shift in 62 games just 54 seconds into the first period, centering a line with Boyd Devereaux and Luc Robitaille. He went back to the bench 57 seconds later. At other times, Yzerman played right wing with Kris Draper at center and Kirk Maltby on the left.

▌ **This one is mine:** Yzerman won his first face-off, against the Kings' Erik Rasmussen, sending the puck back to Devereaux.

▌ **Oops, he did it again:** Yzerman got tangled up with Rasmussen on the first face-off and tumbled to the ice, and he fell again during his second shift. His right knee seemed A-OK.

▌ **Everybody hurts, sometimes:** After Brendan Shanahan took a shot right where it hurts the most, Yzerman spent a minute chatting with his old linemate during a TV time-out.

BORN: CRANBROOK, BC, 1965

ADOPTED: DETROIT, MI, 1983

Steve Yzerman. Over 600 goals. 3 Stanley Cup® Championships. And more than 16 years as captain.

ROMAIN BLANQUART

POSTER BOY

BY DAN SHINE

From 2003 to 2005, a 170-by-100-foot mural of Steve Yzerman graced the side of the Cadillac Tower in downtown Detroit, overlooking Campus Martius and Kennedy Square.

The painting of Yzerman, shown bent at the waist resting his stick on his thighs, said: "Born: Cranbrook, BC, 1965. Adopted: Detroit, MI, 1983."

In small print at the bottom, it read: "Steve Yzerman. Over 600 goals. 3 Stanley Cup Championships. And more than 16 years as captain."

The push to put Yzerman on the building began after the Wings' Stanley Cup victory in 2002. Nextel, a Red Wings sponsor that had purchased the rights to advertise on the wall, was interested in doing something with the team.

While discussions with Yzerman started, the wireless company decided to put up a painting of the Stanley Cup. Coinciding with that was a grassroots campaign and petition drive by fans to have the image of Yzerman grace the building. Organizers collected thousands of signatures.

A Nextel vice president said the mural was a tribute to "hockey's greatest fans" and to Yzerman, "Detroit's hockey legend."

Artists Art Pastusak and Jason Coatney, of Portland, Ore., began the project after 30 gallons of white paint were used to cover the Stanley Cup. They spent two days putting the outline and features of Yzerman's image on the wall.

Before traveling to Detroit, Coatney projected Yzerman's picture on a wall at his home in 4-by-8-foot sections.

Using sections of paper, Coatney then traced the outline and nuances of the image on the wall with a special pen that burned a hole in the paper wherever he touched it.

Like a puzzle, these dozens of numbered papers were affixed to the building wall and dusted with charcoal powder so it left a traceable pattern.

Then the painting began. First the winged wheel jersey and pants, and then Yzerman's battle-scarred face.

"Doing the face was a blast," Coatney said.

Added Pastusak: "That's when you have to be an artist."

The men combined enamel paint and a paste mix to get the right consistency.

Reds and whites were combined to give Yzerman's face some contrast against the stucco facade and "to make his gloves look like leather," Pastusak said.

They used brushes and rollers. In all, about 100 gallons of paint were used to complete the mural.

Darren McCarty said it was a fitting tribute to Yzerman.

"He embodies the city," McCarty said. "He's a larger-than-life figure."

CAPT-IVATING OPENER: OCTOBER 10, 2003

BY MITCH ALBOM

Now that's how you start a season — with a perfect finish. The final rush, game tied and a surging Steve Yzerman, in the first game of 2003, takes a sweet backhand pass from his newest teammate, Ray Whitney, and zaps it past the L.A. goalie for the victory. He slaps the ice with his stick, shakes both fists toward the heavens, and smiles with every inch of the white mouth guard that protects his teeth, looking up, in amazement, at the frozen digits on the scoreboard: 1.7 seconds.

For one night, anyhow, The Captain beat back time.

"Is that the happiest you've been in a while over a goal?" someone asked Yzerman, after his game-winner gave the Red Wings a 3-2 opening-night victory over the Los Angeles Kings.

"Well, it's been a good 18 months since I did something like that," he said, grinning.

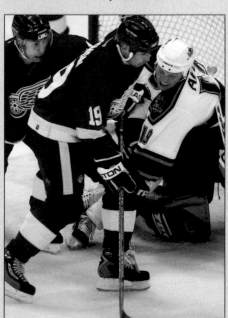

KIRTHMON F. DOZIER

His only shot of the night? The last shot of the game? In the net? Game over?

It was the reason Yzerman captured the imagination of every sports fan in Detroit, and the reason why no one gave up on him and he didn't give up on himself.

During the exhibition season, he felt "slow." His surgically repaired right knee was not bouncing back the way he wanted it to. Scoring wasn't his concern. Skating was. Before the opener, he received a tremendous ovation from the fans.

"What did you think of that?" someone asked.

He shook his head and chuckled. "I was just hoping it didn't turn to boos by the third period."

Not a chance. He beat the goalie. He beat the clock. He beat his own self-doubt.

That's a finish.

KING ME: Yzerman and L.A.'s Sean Avery fight for the puck during the 2003 season opener at the Joe. Yzerman went on to score the winning goal with 1.7 seconds left, jump-starting the season in exciting fashion.

A BED, A DRESSER, A DREAM SET

To be honest, it looks like the kind of perfectly normal furniture you might see in the bedroom of a mentally stable person.

PULL UP A CHAIR: The Captain's furniture is adorned with tiny metal plates that say "Steve Yzerman Collection."

ART VAN FURNITURE

BY MICHAEL ROSENBERG

2004
APRIL 26

So what would you pay to sleep in Steve Yzerman's bed?

Wait! Let me clarify.

Art Van Furniture is selling the Steve Yzerman Collection of bedroom furniture. The store has sold many of its sets for kids, which is understandable.

But the Yzerman collection also comes in an adult set, which is disturbing.

Not to judge those who would purchase such a thing, but just to see what kind of sick weirdo would do it.

The bed is not made of hockey sticks. It does not feature some new, patented "gap-toothed" technology.

To be honest, it looks like the kind of perfectly normal furniture you might see in the bedroom of a mentally stable person. It's a tasteful, subdued wood, without a trace

of red paint. There are no winged wheels. Only the little metal "Steve Yzerman Collection" plates mark it as property of a lunatic Wings fan.

The Yzerman collection includes a dresser (for jockstraps and such), nightstands (for that digitally created photo of you and Stevie Y) and a mirror. If you want a red light to go off when the bed shakes, you have to install it yourself.

Athletes have pitched stranger products. Remember that awful Michael Jordan cologne? See that sweaty man? For the right price, you can smell just like him!

Then there is the Viagra endorsement of baseball star Rafael Palmeiro. In a normal, mature society, this would not be a big deal, but Palmeiro played a sport in which grown men are supposed to scratch themselves and spit while they're working.

Here's another problem with the Steve Yzerman bedroom collection. It violates the Cynical Fan's First Rule: Never spend too much money on something with an athlete's name on it. It's too risky.

You buy a fancy luggage set from a Hall of Fame quarterback, and pretty soon he's arrested for carrying a gun and cocaine onto a plane.

Admittedly, Yzerman appears to be the safest bet in the world to stay out of trouble, and it's easier to picture George W. Bush as a Democrat than Yzerman playing for another team.

But a rule is a rule.

If a guy gets traded, you can hang his jersey in the closet. If he commits a felony, you can roll up his poster and throw it in the trash.

What are these folks going to do if Yzerman does something wrong? Sleep on the floor? ○

SITTING PRETTY: Off the ice, Yzerman dabbles in the furniture-making business — fear not, no hockey sticks were harmed in the making of his products. His collection is sold at Art Van Furniture and caters to kids, adults and collectors of all things Hockeytown.

ART VAN FURNITURE

CAREER IN JEOPARDY

"When I saw his legs kicking, I knew it was bad."
Teammate Brendan Shanahan

It's cold, it's hard, it's dangerous and it flies. And when a puck hits an unprotected hockey player, it takes no prisoners, it simply destroys, a tooth, a jaw, a cheekbone, a piece of the skull.

An eye.

BY MITCH ALBOM

2004
MAY 1

Brendan Shanahan saw the puck that hit his friend and teammate Steve Yzerman, saw it lift The Captain like a gunshot, then drop him limp on the ice. He saw Yzerman try to scramble to his feet, then fall down again, and Shanahan's stomach tightened.

"When I saw his legs kicking, I knew it was bad," Shanahan said. "Steve is a guy who never embellishes an injury, and we all know he has a pretty high threshold for pain. When I saw his legs kicking, I had to go out and see what happened."

What happened, we now know, was this: The small, rubber demon struck Yzerman in the face, smashing his left eye socket, scratching his cornea and sending him to 4½ hours of surgery.

"When we got into the locker room, everybody was asking, 'How bad was it?'" Shanahan said. "At that moment, whether he's going to play isn't even a thought. An eye is a lot more important than whether Steve plays in the next game."

Shanahan, with Robert Lang, helped lead Yzerman off the ice. His eye was covered in a towel. There was no visible blood. Viewers feared the worst.

Reporters whispered about the damage. And players like Shanahan, who dart around the flying rubber demon every night, flashed back on the hits and near-misses of their careers.

"I took a puck in the face when I was 21 and with New Jersey," Shanahan said. "Not as bad as Steve's, but it broke my cheekbone, my orbital bone.

"You don't have any time to get out of the way. I've seen it happen many times, where it's just a matter of an inch this way or that way.

"I know it doesn't sound lucky, when we're talking about Steve, but

DAVID P. GILKEY

ACHES AND PAINS: An eye injury in 2004 and countless other setbacks plagued Yzerman during the twlight of his career.

we're all just thankful he doesn't have permanent damage."

There was no measuring what Yzerman must have been feeling. His storied resilience was well known. He weathered knee injuries and groin injuries and shoulder injuries. He weathered operation after operation, one before the 2002-03 season that was so grisly — sawing into a bone and inserting a wedge — it almost seemed barbaric.

But always there was a comeback night at Joe Louis Arena, when the lights lowered and the locker-room door was opened and he stepped onto the ice and skated a circle — and the roof threatened to blow off from the noise.

Still, Yzerman knew those nights were limited, that you get only so many in a career. He downplayed his "hello agains" for a reason; he didn't want to exaggerate his good-bye. ●

TO RUSSIA, WITH LOVE

CLASS REUNION: Yzerman, along with teammate Tomas Holmstrom, left, were reunited with Slava Fetisov during an exhibition game in Moscow during the lockout season. Fetisov's all-Russian team defeated an all-world team, featuring Yzerman, 6-5.

MOSCOW — For one night, anyway, Moscow was Hockeytown.

With the NHL in the throes of a lockout, 33 players got together to play some big-time, soft-checking hockey in a farewell game honoring Russian legend Igor Larionov.

BY MARK McDONALD

2004
DECEMBER 14

Larionov, a three-time Stanley Cup winner with the Red Wings, retired after the 2003-04 season but invited some of his old pals to Moscow for an exhibition. Many of them were current or former Wings, plus coaches Scotty Bowman, Dave Lewis and Barry Smith.

The game ended in a 6-5 victory for Larionov's all-Russian squad over a world team captained by Steve Yzerman. Fittingly, Larionov scored a goal, assisted by former Wing Sergei Fedorov, against goaltender Chris Osgood.

After the second period, Larionov and Yzerman switched teams. Yzerman then scored twice in his biggest test since he suffered an eye injury May 1, 2004, during the Wings' playoff series with Calgary.

Russian Prime Minister Mikhail Fradkov attended the Larionov farewell, played before a sellout crowd at the Luzhniki sports complex. President Vladimir Putin was invited but didn't show; instead, he sent over a green-ribboned Order of Friendship.

Larionov said the game left him with "bittersweet feelings."

"It was a sad day and a great day," he said. "I am happy that so many friends and so many former Detroit Red Wings came to play."

Yzerman, whose only previous visit to Russia was in 1983 for the world junior championships, had considered not coming to the farewell game. But his affection for

Larionov persuaded him.

"It was just a fun game, and it was nice to see Igor get a goal," Yzerman said. "But the little celebration on the ice after the game took on a different meaning — a little bit sad. I don't think any of us like to think about retiring."

It was a nostalgic evening as well for Slava Fetisov, the former Wings defenseman who became the head of the Russian sports federation. He helped pioneer the way for Soviet players to play in Europe and the NHL. He and Larionov left the legendary Red Army team for the NHL in 1989.

Eventually, they made their way to Detroit, where they prospered under Bowman.

"Those championships were a direct result of the Russian players coming to our team," Bowman said. "They gave us something nobody could have dreamed of." Ⓒ

RETIREMENT ON HOLD

Yzerman had serious discussions with the Red Wings about retiring in late November 2005.

KIRTHMON F. DOZIER

STICKING AROUND: Yzerman stands his ground in front of the net against Calgary goalie Miikka Kiprusoff and Robyn Regehr. Before a change of heart, Yzerman had planned Detroit's game against Calgary on Dec. 1, 2005, to be his last.

Steve Yzerman came close to retiring in the middle of the 2005-06 season. A lot closer than most people realize.

How close?

BY MICHAEL ROSENBERG One game away.

According to two people familiar with his thinking, Yzerman had serious discussions with the Red Wings about retiring in late November 2005. He even had a final game in mind: Dec. 1 at home against Calgary.

When the Wings played Nov. 26 at San Jose, Yzerman took the highly unusual step of asking out of the lineup.

"My knee was sore," Yzerman said then. "I just wanted to take a day off, just to rest."

That was only part of the story. Though nobody knew it, Yzerman had been hit in the head against Anaheim the night before. The combination of the head injury and his knee troubles were too much to overcome.

Yzerman was frustrated by his inability to make plays he made just two or three years earlier. And to Yzerman's disappointment, the Wings' new coach, Mike Babcock, did not seem to have much faith in his star. While predecessors

Scotty Bowman and Dave Lewis were deferential to Yzerman, Babcock was not.

Babcock had given Yzerman only 6 minutes, 37 seconds of ice time against Anaheim. The game before that, his ice time was 6:17.

Yzerman understandably did not want to be a six-minute-per-night player. But he seemed stuck in that role. Two other Wings centers were thriving: Pavel Datsyuk's playmaking style seemed perfect for the new NHL, and Robert Lang had five assists in the San Jose game alone.

Then came an ironic twist: Instead of retiring because of injury, Yzerman avoided retirement because of an injury.

It was the night of Nov. 28, two days after Yzerman asked out of the lineup. The Wings were playing at Los Angeles. This was supposed to be Yzerman's final road game. It changed his season instead.

Early in the second period, Lang suffered a groin injury. Less than five minutes later, Yzerman assisted on a Mathieu Schneider goal. A few minutes after that, The Captain followed up with a goal of his own.

With Lang out of the lineup, Babcock had no choice but to give Yzerman more ice time. And with his performance against L.A. (he nearly scored two other times), Yzerman suddenly had reason to think he could play at a high level again.

The Wings came home for that Dec. 1 game against Calgary. But Yzerman's retirement was now on hold. He continued to improve, and in the last month, Yzerman was one of the Wings' best players — a development that seemed impossible just a few months before. ⊙

NEW WORLD ORDER: Red Wings coach Mike Babcock, yelling instructions to his players, limited Yzerman's playing time during the early stages of the 2005-06 season. But when Robert Lang was injured Nov. 28 against the Los Angeles Kings, Yzerman earned more minutes by scoring a goal and making an assist.

JULIAN H. GONZALEZ

THE LAST GAME

EDMONTON, Alberta — In the end, the Red Wings lost this series because the rest of the team could not follow the example set by their nearly 41-year-old captain.

BY HELENE ST. JAMES

2006

MAY 1

Steve Yzerman shrugged off a torn rib muscle and almost breathed life back into the Wings, skating hard, setting up a goal, and nearly willing his team back into this first-round series. But in the end, neither their offense nor their defense nor their goaltending came through, and so once again the Wings left the playoffs earlier than expected, upset by the eighth-seeded Oilers.

The Wings lost, 4-3, to Edmonton at Rexall Place in what turned out to be Yzerman's last game.

After the game, he focused on what went wrong after the Wings finished with the best record in the regular season only to flop in the playoffs.

"It's happened to us a couple of times where we've had very good regular seasons and a lot of lofty goals for the playoffs," he said. "It's disappointing. They made some good plays to score a couple goals."

The Wings blew a two-goal lead and then a one-goal lead in the third period, beaten twice by Fernando Pisani and then twice by Ales Hemsky, the last with 1:06 left in the game.

"We went out and played a great first two periods, probably the best two periods of the whole series, and then we sat back on our heels, which is a no-no," Mathieu Schneider said. "It's very disappointing and shocking."

The Wings went home because of a third period in which they melted and the Oilers caught fire. At 2:56, Pisani hammered Jarret Stoll's rebound into an open net. Pisani scored again at 6:40, when he slipped a backhand shot underneath Manny Legace. It was the beginning of the end for Legace, for the Wings and for Yzerman's legendary career.

"He could be the toughest guy I've ever played with," Schneider said of Yzerman. "He was in definite pain the last few days. I for one never thought he was going to play tonight and he goes out and continues to amaze." ◯

PHOTOS BY JULIAN H. GONZALEZ

LEGEND OF THE FALL: Yzerman is taken down by Edmonton's Dick Tarnstrom during Game 6 of the first-round playoff series. Yzerman played with a torn rib muscle, proving once again he wouldn't be subdued by pain.

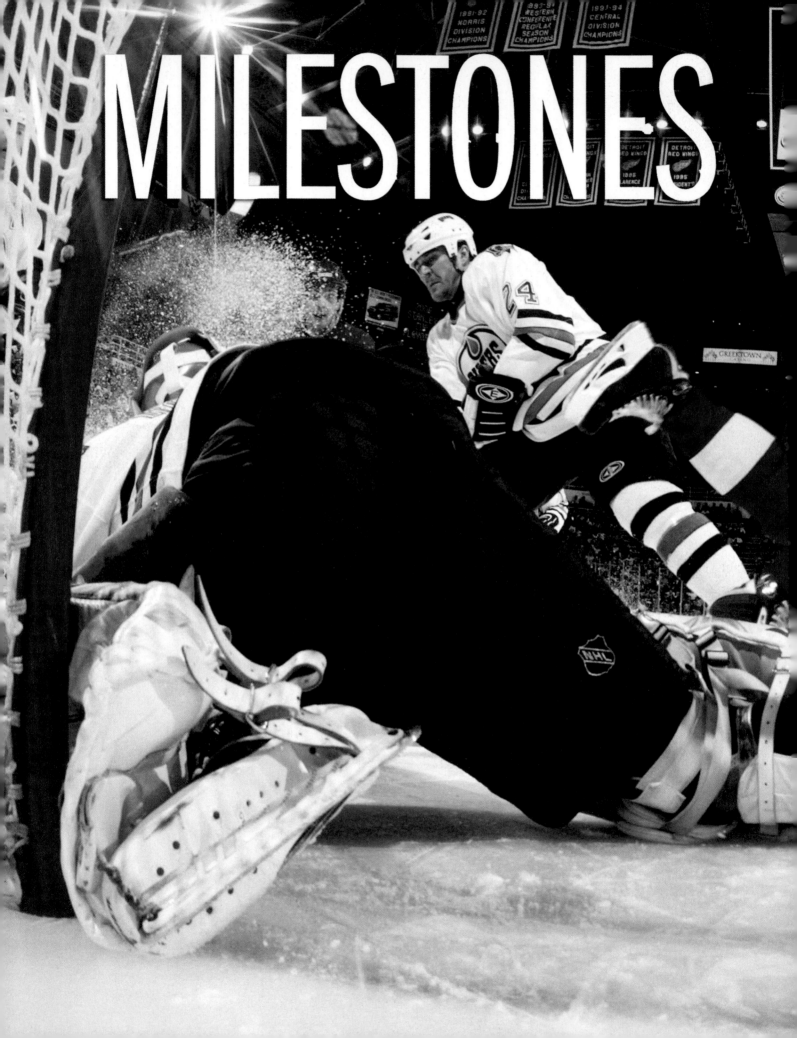

MILESTONES

THE FIRST ONE

▮ **Oct. 5, 1983, at Winnipeg:** Yzerman scored the Wings' third goal in a 6-6 tie, the season opener and his first game as an 18-year-old rookie. He fought off two checks and skated diagonally through the Jets' zone, beating goalie Doug Soetart on his own rebound.

FIRST HAT TRICK

▮ **Dec. 23, 1983, vs. Toronto:** Young Yzerman and veteran John Ogrodnick each scored three times against Maple Leafs goalie Mike Palmateer in a 9-2 win at the Joe.

100TH GOAL

▮ **Jan. 17, 1987, vs. Quebec:** Yzerman scored the 100th of his career in the second period of a 3-2 win over the Nordiques. He grabbed a rebound in the left face-off circle, skated through the defense to the right corner, faked goalie Clint Malarchuk to the ice and flipped the puck into the upper-left corner of the net. Ogrodnick got an assist on the goal and was traded to Quebec after the game.

FIRST 50-GOAL SEASON

▮ **March 1, 1988, vs. Buffalo:** Yzerman became the fourth Wing to score 50 goals in a season when his backhand from the right corner beat the Sabres' Tom Barrasso — who had edged Yzerman for rookie of the year in 1984 — in a 4-0 victory. Yzerman retrieved the puck, skated toward his bench and flung it into the crowd. But the Joe was silenced later in the game when Yzerman, 22, slid into the goal post and had to be carried off the ice with a right knee injury. "My heart went from where it was supposed to be down to my toes, and I think it's still there," general manager Jimmy Devellano said after the game. Yzerman missed the final 16 games of the regular season and the first two rounds of the playoffs, returning for the final three games of the conference finals against Edmonton.

200TH GOAL

▮ **Dec. 30, 1988, at Hartford:** Yzerman beat Mike Liut for his 200th career goal in a 4-3 loss to the Whalers.

THE CAPTAIN: 22 seasons, 692 goals.

JULIAN H. GONZALEZ

65-GOAL SEASON

Key moments in Yzerman's team-record 65-goal season in 1988-89:

■ **Feb. 21, 1989, vs. N.Y. Islanders:** Yzerman beat Kelly Hrudey twice, including the winner in a 6-5 victory, tying John Ogrodnick's team record of 55 goals in a season (and, with an assist, got his 123rd point, breaking Marcel Dionne's team record of 121). On the second goal, Yzerman said defenseman Richard Pilon "had my hands tied up. I just sort of directed it toward the net. I was able to get a weak shot off, and it went off the post and in. I got lucky."

■ **Feb. 23, 1989, vs. Pittsburgh:** Yzerman scored twice in a 6-6 tie — including the tying goal with five minutes left, completing a comeback from a 6-0 deficit — breaking and extending the record to 57 goals. The record-breaking goal came on a wrist shot from between the circles midway through the second period, making it 6-2. "I wasn't too thrilled about it at the time," Yzerman said after the game. "We were down, 6-0. It was embarrassing, especially at home. You want to do something, if you have any pride in yourself." On the tying goal, Yzerman was trying to pass to Paul MacLean, but the puck wound up slithering past Barrasso. Said MacLean: "I don't know how Barrasso missed it."

■ **April 2, 1989, at St. Louis:** Yzerman got his 65th goal — still the Wings' record — in the season finale, a 4-2 loss to the Blues. His 90 assists and 155 points that season also are team records.

300TH GOAL

■ **Nov. 1, 1990, vs. Toronto:** Yzerman beat Peter Ing in the second period for the 300th goal of his career in a 5-4 win over the Maple Leafs. "If I play long enough, I guess that's going to happen," Yzerman said. But he was appreciative of the two-minute standing ovation the Joe Louis Arena crowd gave him: "It was unexpected. But it was nice to sit on the bench and hear that." Yzerman also was asked if he got as much satisfaction from keeping the Leafs penned in their zone in the game's final seconds. "Ummm, not really," he said. "Checkers don't make very much money."

GOALS

400TH GOAL

▪ **Nov. 13, 1992, vs. Pittsburgh:** Yzerman beat Barrasso again for his 400th career goal and also added No. 401 in an 8-0 win over the Penguins, the two-time defending Stanley Cup champions.

500TH GOAL

▪ **Jan. 17, 1996, vs. Colorado:** Yzerman became the 22nd player in NHL history to score 500 goals when he grabbed his own rebound and beat Patrick Roy with a backhander in a 3-2 win. "Simply happiness," Yzerman said when asked how it felt. "I didn't feel relief at all because I've been enjoying all the buildup leading up to it the last couple of weeks. It's been something I've really enjoyed." Among those congratulating Yzerman in the Detroit dressing room was team co-owner Marian Ilitch, who greeted him with a kiss: "I'm so proud of you. I can remember the day we drafted you and you were wearing that little red tie. It seems like only yesterday."

MOST MEMORABLE GOAL

▪ **May 16, 1996, vs. St. Louis:** This is the Yzerman goal that makes all the Wings' highlight reels, the 55-foot slapshot off the crossbar that beat Blues goalie Jon Casey 1:15 into the second overtime for a 1-0 win in Game 7 of the Western Conference semifinals. "I don't score a whole lot from the blue line, so I was definitely surprised," Yzerman said. "I shot it and looked up and heard the clang against the bar and I was like, 'No way. It went in.'... "It's the kind of goal every player dreams about in his career."

600TH GOAL

▪ **Nov. 26, 1999, vs. Edmonton:** Yzerman became the 11th player to score 600 goals with a little help from Oilers goalie Tommy Salo in a 4-2 win. It wasn't exactly one for the highlight reels. "I just picked up a loose puck," Yzerman said. "I was looking for (Slava Kozlov), the goalie reached out to block the pass and it re-directed in off his glove. I don't know if I deserved it, but I'm taking it. ... Ideally, I would have drawn it up a little prettier than that. But I've gotten some lousy goals over the years, too." As far as reaching that milestone, he said: "I don't really use that as a barometer. I just kind of play. That's a total of the last 17 years, and it doesn't really matter at this point."

THE LAST ONE

▪ **April 3, 2006, at Calgary:** Yzerman's 692nd and final goal was the Wings' only regulation score in a 2-1 shootout win over the Flames. He beat Miikka Kiprusoff after Pavel Datsyuk won a face-off in the Calgary zone. Yzerman, 40, played four more games in the regular season and four in the playoffs, but he did not score a goal.

UPS AND DOWNS: Yzerman was awarded the Masterton Trophy after missing 66 games during the 2002-03 season.
KIRTHMON F. DOZIER

ROOKIE OF THE YEAR?

Not quite. Yzerman led all rookies in scoring with 48 assists and 87 points but was a runner-up to Buffalo goalie Tom Barrasso in voting for the Calder Trophy.

That vote was by hockey writers. Yzerman was The Sporting News rookie of the year in a vote by NHL players, and he was named to the league's all-rookie team.

THE YOUNGEST ALL-STAR

Yzerman, 18, was the youngest player ever named to the NHL All-Star Game and the only rookie in the 1984 match.

"It's great for the club to have two players in the game, but I'd just as soon be in the playoffs," Yzerman said. "Really, my only goal at the beginning of the season was to make the playoffs. That's everybody's goal in Detroit, so I'd gladly trade it."

In the game, Yzerman assisted on a goal by fellow Red Wing John Ogrodnick in a 7-6 loss for the Campbell Conference.

"I certainly won't forget the game," Yzerman said. "I got it on videotape. I'll go home and just sit down and watch it every now and then."

He was named to the All-Star Game 10 times and played in nine.

THE CAPTAIN

On Oct. 7, 1986, needing a successor for Danny Gare, coach Jacques Demers made the 21-year-old Yzerman the Red Wings' youngest captain. In 2006, Yzerman retired as the NHL's longest-serving captain.

OUTSTANDING!

It seems a crime, but Yzerman never won or even was a runner-up for the Hart Trophy as the league MVP. But in 1989, he did win the Lester B. Pearson Award as the NHL's outstanding player in a vote by the players' association.

Mario Lemieux was second and Wayne Gretzky third, and the same three were finalists for the Hart that season. Gretzky won it and Lemieux was second in the vote by hockey writers.

Yzerman also was voted player of the year by Hockey News readers after his 65-goal, 155-point season. He was in Toronto for all the award ceremonies, even though it was his and Lisa's wedding week in June 1989.

"The only lines I had rehearsed were my wedding vows," he said in accepting the Hockey News award. "I have been very busy and haven't thought much about hockey but really am looking forward to my wedding and honeymoon."

SELKE TROPHY

Yzerman's evolution as a player was demonstrated by his winning of the 2000 Selke Trophy as the league's top defensive forward. He scored 35 goals and 79 points and was named a first-team All-Star, along with teammates Brendan Shanahan and Nicklas Lidstrom.

THE GOLDEN YEAR

Yzerman represented his native country in several international tournaments, most notably the 1998 Nagano Olympics and the 2002 Salt Lake Games. Canada won the gold in '02 and the Wings won the Stanley Cup a few months later, making Yzerman, teammate Brendan Shanahan and Davison's Ken Morrow (USA's Miracle on Ice in 1980, N.Y. Islanders) the only players to complete that double in the same year.

Yzerman was asked to play at Torino in 2006, but when he bowed out because of injury, executive director Wayne Gretzky retired his No. 19.

MASTERTON TROPHY

Yzerman, who missed the first 66 games of the 2002-03 season while recovering from knee surgery, won the Masterton Trophy for perseverance, sportsmanship and dedication to hockey.

"Usually I don't agree with what the media says, but I think they finally got one right here," Yzerman joked. "I've played a long time, and I've had a lot of ups and downs, and I'd like to think it isn't just because I had knee surgery and came back and played this year. I've had several — whether it's physical or other — setbacks in playing the game."

JULIAN H. GONZALEZ

TEAM PLAYER: Yzerman finished his career with 1,063 assists.

1,000TH POINT

▪ **Nov. 1, 1990, at Buffalo:** After giving back his 1,000th point in the previous game because he said he didn't deserve an assist, Yzerman got it back with a helper on Keith Primeau's first-period goal in a 10-7 loss. The loss spoiled the night for Yzerman, who finished with a goal and three assists: "It's not sad, but it's kind of tough to enjoy, really. We played poorly, and I thought I played poorly. So I don't know how you can do that and enjoy reaching any type of milestone. "I can't say reaching 1,000 points was something I set out to do. It's really a nice accomplishment, but there are other things I want to do. In particular, I always wanted to play on a great team and win a Stanley Cup. I mean, this is really nice. But it probably won't be until next year, or maybe next week after a good game, that I'll really enjoy it."

1,000TH GAME

▪ **Feb. 19, 1997, vs. Calgary:** In his 1,000th game — all with the Wings, of course — Yzerman had three assists in a 4-0 win. "It's a neat thing to do," he said. "I don't know how many guys have done it all with one team. It gives you a chance to reflect on different situations that you've been in. I've played with a lot of guys and been through a lot here. It's all been in Detroit, but I feel like I've been on four or five different teams here."

1,000TH ASSIST

▪ **Jan. 20, 2002, vs. Ottawa:** Yzerman became the ninth NHL player with 1,000 assists when he set up Mathieu Dandenault's overtime goal in a 3-2 win over the Senators. "I have a lot of respect for the guys who have reached that," he said. "But I look at it that I've played a long time on a good team with a lot of good players, and it's slowly added up. So I don't really look at it as any great achievement. ... We won the Stanley Cup, and those two blow everything else away. For the first 12-13 years of my career, I was getting all these points, and it wasn't good enough, and I recognized that. We've got to win, we've got to win — everybody thought the same thing. We were able to do that. It's the same thing now. Winning is more exciting than the milestones."

1,024TH ASSIST

▪ **Jan. 6, 2004, vs. Nashville:** Yzerman's assist on Kris Draper's first-period goal in a 6-0 win was the 1,024th of his career, breaking Gordie Howe's Wings record. "I guess I'm a little surprised," Yzerman said. "I didn't expect to catch him on any lists." Yzerman finished his career with 1,063 assists. He and Howe are 1-2 on the Wings' other major scoring lists: Howe leads in goals, 786-692, and in points, 1,809-1,755.

1,050TH ASSIST

▪ **Jan. 12, 2006, vs. Philadelphia:** Yzerman's assist on Robert Lang's goal — the Red Wings' fifth in the third period of a 6-3 win — moved Yzerman ahead of Howe for seventh place on the NHL all-time assist list. Howe had 1,049 assists in 1,767 games. "To be passing Gordie Howe — holy mackerel!" coach Mike Babcock said. "That's unbelievable. That's how good you've been and that's how long you've played. And that's how good of players you played with." When public address announcer Budd Lynch told the Joe Louis Arena crowd that Yzerman had passed Howe, the fans clapped and began chanting, "Stevie! Stevie!"

ALL ABOARD: Yzerman roughs it up during the **2002 playoffs.**

JULIAN H. GONAZLEZ

TRIBUTES

STEVIE TIME

"The bigger the game, the better he played."

Teammate Kris Draper

ERIC SEALS

O CAPTAIN! MY CAPTAIN: After 22 seasons, 19 as captain, Steve Yzerman will be remembered for his leadership.

Ty Cobb once was voted the best baseball player of the first half of the 20th Century — ahead of Babe Ruth.

Gordie Howe often is called, matter-of-factly, the best all-around hockey player.

Barry Sanders was arguably the best player ever at arguably the most important position in football.

Isiah Thomas is considered the best little man in NBA history.

Steve Yzerman made the All-NHL first team only once.

BY MICHAEL ROSENBERG

And yet, when we speak of Detroit sports icons, Yzerman is near the top of the list.

Yzerman's stature is not just about performance, although his was exceptional. (He missed out on All-NHL honors because he played the same position, in the same era, as Wayne Gretzky and Mario Lemieux.) Yzerman has a mystique that can largely be explained by what he didn't do.

He did not change teams. (Heck, in the age of marketing idiocy, when teams get new logos every few years, he did not even change uniforms.) He did not intimidate rookies for his own amusement. He did not get arrested. He did not ask to get out of Detroit. He did not moan about

his salary. He did not complain terribly when people said he was a great player but had never won a Stanley Cup.

He did not bristle when former Red Wings coach Scotty Bowman asked him to play better defense — instead, he adapted and won the Selke Trophy as the league's best defensive forward. He did not seek attention but did not whine when he got it. When Yzerman spoke to reporters, he did not always say something memorable, but he also did not ever say anything stupid.

Yzerman's most celebrated trait is leadership. His job description and nickname are one and the same:

The Captain.

But even in that role, he was effective largely because of what he did not do.

"You can't just have somebody talking every day," Bowman said. "He didn't do that."

Yzerman was asked when he retired after 22 seasons, 19 as captain, to name his greatest accomplishment. Fittingly, he did not pick one. This allows others to see what they want to see, to remember what they wish to remember.

And what will we remember most? In 1997, Yzerman led the Wings to their first Stanley Cup in 42 years, ending the longest drought in the NHL. In 1998, he won the Conn Smythe Trophy as playoff MVP. Logically, any Yzerman remembrance should start with those two achievements. But for people who watched Yzerman up close, the enduring memory is of the 2002 Stanley Cup run, when he did not give in to the agonizing pain in his right knee.

"Not being able to pregame skate through the entire playoffs, not being able to practice through the playoffs and after every game his knee just swelling up — he basically had ice bags from his ankle all the way up to his hip to settle the swelling down," Kris Draper said.

When he got knocked to the ice that spring, Yzerman had to lean on his left knee to lift himself up.

"Just getting through that was really a struggle for me," Yzerman said. "Sometimes I thought I was effective. Other times I thought I was just buying time out there."

Yzerman scored 23 points in 23 playoff games that year.

No other Wing scored more than 19.

"The bigger the game, the better he played," Draper said. "Even the little things: When you needed a face-off, Stevie was the guy who was going to win that face-off."

Those 2002 Wings had one of the most star-laden teams in sports history: nine likely Hall of Famers on the roster, and a coach, Bowman, who already had been inducted. Yet there was never any doubt that it was Yzerman's team.

"Absolutely," Draper said. "We knew. Even when Brett Hull comes in, Luc Robitaille, Dominik Hasek, those guys knew that they were coming to play for the Detroit Red Wings, and Steve Yzerman was the man. Those players were going to show Stevie. I think that's why everything worked out as well as it did."

There is a story about the

LEGEND: Yzerman brought the Stanley Cup to Detroit three times, in 1997, 1998 and 2002.

JULIAN H. GONZALEZ

STEVIE TIME

BINGO BANGO: Yzerman tucks the puck behind Blackhawks netminder Nikolai Khabibulin.

JULIAN H. GONZALEZ

2002 playoffs that has become a staple of all tributes to Yzerman. In the first round against Vancouver, the Wings lost the first two games at home. Then Yzerman gave a speech, the team won four straight and went on to win the Stanley Cup.

It is the stuff of Disney movies. But Yzerman was never a Disney-movie kind of leader, and he barely remembers the speech. When Brendan Shanahan asked Yzerman if he would address the team before Game 3, Yzerman replied, "I don't think so."

"And he said, 'Maybe you should say something,'" Yzerman recalled. "'OK, I guess so.' What effect it has on players, I really don't know."

What Yzerman does remember is the crushing pain in his knee and the sense that his career might end at any moment. After warm-ups before Game 2 against Vancouver, Yzerman went back to the Wings' dressing room and told Bowman he didn't think he could play.

"I was hoping he would say, 'That's OK, don't worry — we'll go with somebody else,'" Yzerman said. "He just said, 'Do what you can do.' And I was kind of like, 'Uh-oh.'

"We went and we lost, and at that point I'm like, 'I can't bail out now.'"

The Yzerman Wings were notorious for avoiding the media after games. Newspaper readers were treated to a seemingly endless string of quotes from Darren McCarty, a player of limited ability, simply because McCarty was happy to answer questions while his teammates stayed away.

This, too, was Yzerman's influence: The Captain spoke only when necessary. But after that Game 2 loss to Vancouver, it was necessary. Yzerman quickly made himself available, calmly answered every question, then limped slowly out of Joe Louis Arena.

A few weeks later, he was playing in the Stanley Cup finals, reminding himself to enjoy it because his career was probably ending.

"I didn't want to retire, but I thought, 'Oh, my God,'" Yzerman said. "I didn't really understand at the time what I was doing. I was just saying, 'If this doesn't get any better, there is no way I can play next year.'"

It got a little better, after he had an osteotomy on his knee, a radical procedure designed more to extend the knee's life than to help him get back on the ice. Yzerman said that, in his mind, his career ended in 2002. After that, he relied mostly on toughness and brains.

Yet even on nights when he could barely skate and did not speak publicly, Yzerman was the face of this team. In media sessions, Yzerman gave long, thoughtful answers and therefore controlled the pace of the conversation. This was how he played, too. Early in his career, Yzerman was one of the best scorers in the world, but by the end, his greatest gift was holding the puck — extending a play, avoiding the opponents and looking around the ice until he could feed a teammate for a scoring chance. In games and in interviews, everything happened on Stevie Time.

Yzerman would like to run a team someday. He says that unless he is playing with his daughters, he has no intention of playing hockey again. Steve Yzerman as a nostalgia act is just one more thing the public won't see.

Somehow, the memories will be more vivid that way.●

"The hardest thing to be is the captain. He wore that 'C' with pride. ... He tried to impress everybody every shift."
GORDIE HOWE

"He's got a good pain tolerance. When an athlete has that, it does give them an extra year or two in his career. ... He's just been a great example, to me, to what an athlete should be. It's the end of an era."
TED LINDSAY, FORMER RED WINGS TOUGH GUY

"He was the face of the Red Wings for the past 20 years and will be remembered as one of the best players and leaders who ever played the game of hockey."
WAYNE GRETZKY, HOCKEY GREAT AND PHOENIX COYOTES COACH

"When I was looking for a captain, I wanted a guy with the Red Wings crest tattooed on his chest. Steve Yzerman was that guy.
JACQUES DEMERS, FORMER RED WINGS COACH

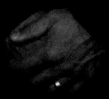

IN GOOD COMPANY: When Yzerman announced his retirement July 3, 2006, members of the Wings' A-list came to wish him well. Former greats Ted Lindsay, left, and Gordie Howe were there, along with former head coach Scotty Bowman, right.

JULIAN H. GONZALEZ

"Steve was a great ambassador for the game and will be sorely missed by everyone associated with the NHL. Steve was a great leader, a great teammate and most importantly a great person. I was fortunate to play at the 2002 Olympics with Steve, and we won a gold medal together. It was a memorable experience and something I'll always cherish."
MARIO LEMIEUX, FORMER PITTSBURGH PENGUINS SUPERSTAR

"Stevie talked (at his retirement press conference) for what, a half hour? Yeah, well, he could talk for a week about 23 years (of playing). Not only what took place but, I mean, all the different players and all the different incidents and situations. It's pretty much a lifetime of hockey, is the way I look at it. ... He's proven he's got leadership ability. He's very intelligent. He has a high IQ. So he'll be successful at whatever he does. So, you know Stevie, sky's the limit."
MIKE ILITCH, WINGS OWNER

"When he did say things, it meant a lot. I never had to worry about his work ethic. I never had to worry about if we were both on the same team. I never had to do any coaching with him."

**SCOTTY BOWMAN,
FORMER RED WINGS COACH**

"With his leadership and determination, with his devotion to the team concept, with his refusal to accept anything less than the best, Steve Yzerman became the symbol of the Red Wings' standard of excellence in the modern era. The National Hockey League is grateful for Steve's many contributions to the sport."

GARY BETTMAN, NHL COMMISSIONER

"You can't replace Steve Yzerman."

MIKE BABCOCK, RED WINGS COACH

"He sort of lived every hockey player's dream life professionally. ... If you could script a career, I think that'd be a good start."

DAVE LEWIS, FORMER TEAMMATE AND COACH; BOSTON BRUINS COACH

CHECK HIM OUT: The Captain tussles with Carolina's Bret Hedican during Game 3 of the 2002 Stanley Cup finals in Raleigh, N.C. The Wings won, 3-2, in triple overtime and took a 2-1 series lead.
KIRTHMON F. DOZIER

"His will to win was remarkable. And not that he spoke a lot in the room, but when he did, his timing was great. And when he showed his frustration on the ice, players got the message. His timing was impeccable, even in retiring. It was all about team — it was always that for him — how could he make the team better."

**KEN DANIELS,
RED WINGS TV ANALYST**

"After we won the Cup in '98, in training camp in Traverse City he was the fittest guy in camp. ... There's a guy that could have said, 'This summer belongs to me. We won two Cups.' He could have just sat in his boat and drank beer all summer. But, no, that's definitely not Steve Yzerman's m.o."

**JIM BEDARD, RED WINGS
GOALTENDING COACH**

"As much as you hear about Stevie being a great leader, he was a great person. Just a way about him, you can't help but respect him. He's not looking to get any attention. He's all about the game."

**LUC ROBITAILLE,
FORMER TEAMMATE**

"One of the classiest players I have played with, if not the classiest."
HAROLD SNEPSTS, FORMER TEAMMATE

"When you think of the Red Wings, you think of Stevie, and vice versa."
GERARD GALLANT, FORMER TEAMMATE; COLUMBUS BLUE JACKETS COACH

"He always considered me as being part of the team. Always invited me for photos and things like that. He made that clear years ago. Makes me feel good because I don't know if that goes on all over the league."
AL SOBOTKA, RED WINGS ZAMBONI DRIVER

"He had a great end of the season and way to finish his career. He's got more than just his knee, too. It's just unbelievable that he's got the heart that he's got. His heart sure didn't give up."
DAVID COLLON, WINGS TEAM DOCTOR

MEN OF MERRIMENT: Yzerman and Sergei Fedorov celebrate teammate Brendan Shanahan's second-period goal in Game 5 of the Stanley Cup finals. The Wings won the game, 3-1, at the Joe to clinch the series and regain the Cup in 2002.

MANDI WRIGHT

"There has never been a more respected hockey player to ever play in the National Hockey League than Stevie. I've said it before and I'll say it again. If someone came down from Mars and wanted to know what a hockey player was, I would show him the perfect hockey player: Stevie Wonder Yzerman."

**DON CHERRY,
HOCKEY ANALYST**

"He made us better players, better people."

**KRIS DRAPER,
LONGTIME TEAMMATE**

CENTER ICE: The Red Wings gather on the ice before their 2002 season opener to witness the hoisting of Detroit's 2001-02 championship banner at Joe Louis Arena. It was the team's third championship in six years.

MANDI WRIGHT

When Steve Yzerman announced his retirement, the Free Press asked readers to share their thoughts. There was no shortage of responses.

"I first met Steve in '85 at a picture-and-autograph session at the Southland Mall. I had just turned 10 and Steve and Greg Stefan decided that, despite being scheduled to leave two hours earlier, they would stay and get photos and sign for everyone that was still in line. What is amazing is that he kept that same level of commitment to his fans for the next 21 years. Thank you, Steve."

**Erik Szpyra,
Ft. Lauderdale, Fla.
(formerly of Taylor)**

"I, like many, had hoped this day would never come. Maybe I was being selfish always wanting to see Yzerman on the ice. He has been my hero since I was 11 and saw him playing for the Peterborough Petes. This day was likely the most empty I have ever felt. But I feel fulfilled knowing that I had the pleasure of growing up and watching who I feel was the greatest player ever to wear a Wings jersey. Thanks, Steve, all the best."

Derek Leneeuw, Toronto

"I remember meeting Stevie at Highland Meadows golf course for the Jamie Farr Classic, and I told him I was his biggest fan. He ended up signing four autographs for me, including my Wings hat, which I did not take off for many years. Stevie Y is my Joe Montana."

Danny Gersz, Toledo

"I remember you for the first time when you played for Team Canada at the World Championships in Prague in 1985. I was a 6-year-old then. I liked your play (as much as a

6-year-old kid can), and became a Red Wings fan thanks to you."

**Jiri Hutecka,
Olomouc, Czech Republic**

"Growing up in Wisconsin, we didn't have a hockey team, so I was an avid Wings fan. I started following the Red Wings when I was about 9, and now I'm 19. I even joined our city hockey team and was the only girl on it because I enjoyed watching you so much and watching you work so well with your team. I requested my jersey number to be 19 after you, Stevie. I believed, along with many other Wings fans here, that you were such a classy team leader. Even my uncle Ben, who is a hardcore Colorado Avs fan, believes you to be one of the best captains in sports history."

**Shelly McDonald,
Madison, Wis.**

"My buddies and I used to play NHL hockey on the old Sega Genesis back in the early '90s. Living in Kansas City, Mo., we didn't know a thing about hockey. However, my team of choice became the Detroit Red Wings. They were

fast and had a great player with a peculiar last name — Yzerman. I totally butchered the pronunciation of his name at first. Soon, though, I was spreading the word of Yzerman and the Red Wings to anyone who'd listen. To help non-hockey fans understand who Stevie Y was, I told them he was the George Brett of his team. Then they understood what a clutch player and team leader he was. Thanks for bringing Hockeytown to K.C."

**Fred Briseno,
Kansas City, Mo.**

"I moved to the Dallas area eight years ago. I only lived in Detroit for 18 months, but I have since, and always will, be a Wings fan. I've been to every Stars-Wings game since being here, and the amount of fans who wear their sweaters with your name on it has always astounded me. I remember going to the December game in Dallas this past season, and a Dallas (fan asked), 'Why does every one of you people wear this guy's jersey? What makes him so special?' As I was about to answer, I heard a voice say, 'He's our leader!' Naturally, it was another

Wings fan. That's all that needs to be said about what you have meant to all of us."

**Jason Metko,
Denton, Texas**

"The best part for me as a father was never having to explain to my kids some stupid off-field/ice antics. Thanks, Steve, not just for what you did on the ice, but also for the examples you set for our children in dedication, perseverance, leadership, and grace."

Ed Borus, Bay City

"I've enjoyed and admired his talent, leadership, courage and class. Thanks for the memories! Best wishes to Steve and his family for the future."

**Susan Williams,
Traverse City**

"As a lifelong fan I salute you for your leadership and talent. You wore the 'C' as our Captain, but to me it indicated your true rank: Class!"

**Mike Knisely,
Asheville, N.C.**

"I've heard people say that the happiest day of my life should be my wedding day or birth of a child. That's a bunch o' crap. Seeing you hoist the Cup in '97 and repeating that in '98 in honor of Vladdie will forever be the best days of my life. Thanks for the memories and for being such a classy and gutsy player. Now please stick around in some role to help the Wings win even more Cups."

**Kristin Maloney,
Los Angeles**

"I will miss your courage, your heart, your toughness, your skills and your leadership. You always conducted yourself as a role model on and off the ice. Stevie, you are definitely the heart of Hockeytown."

**Larry Myshock,
Scottsdale, Ariz.**

LASTING IMPRESSION: Yzerman obliges autograph seeker Blake Dowdy during a hospital visit in December 2005.
Facing page: Fans entering Joe Louis Arena show their allegiance to The Captain.

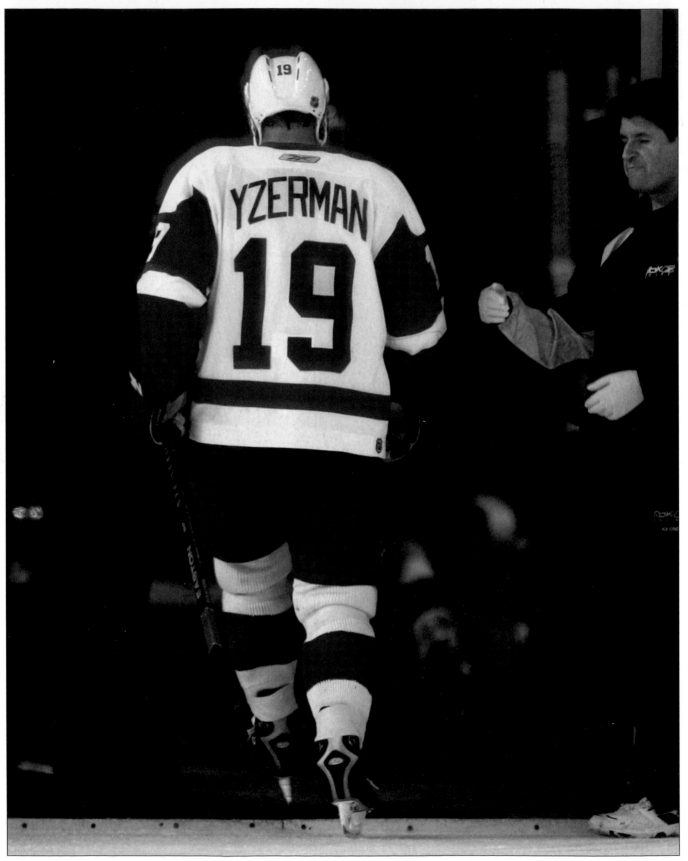

JULIAN H. GONZALEZ